MEMORIES OF
PRESTON

The publishers would like to thank the following companies for their

support in the production of this book

BAKO North Western

R&E Bamford Ltd

E H Booth & Co. Ltd

Chris Miller

Huntapac Produce Ltd

Kirkham Grammar School

Lunar Caravans

Pakawaste Ltd

Sika Limited

J. Wareing & Son (Wrea Green) Ltd

First published in Great Britain by True North Books Limited
England HX3 6SN
01422 244555
www.truenorthbooks.com

MEMORIES OF
PRESTON

CONTENTS

INTRODUCTION

For all of us, memories are the currency which we use to record the changes and progress in our everyday lives and to fix our place as individuals in the greater scheme of things. This is the latest publication in our 'Memories' series of publications, covering nostalgic reflections of towns and cities throughout the UK. In this new book we will be meandering through a pictorial cross-section of life in Preston over the last 100 years or so, to help satisfy the longing we all get from time to time, to recall memories of a different era that now seems better or simpler.

As we get older it is often easier to take a step back, and to view events and developments with a clearer sense of prospective. Our aim has been to assist in this respect by presenting a publication relevant to the area capable of rekindling memories of days gone by in an entertaining and informative manner. Looking through the pages of this book it is interesting to reflect on exactly how much change has taken place in the area over a short period, relative to its long history. Many of these photographs are unique and will inevitably remind us of experiences and events in our lives, of our families and of those whose influence and support has touched us to a greater or lesser degree.

Defining features about nostalgia are universal and can bring back fond memories from a time gone by. Recent research shows that nostalgia can counteract loneliness, boredom and anxiety. Couples feel closer and look happier when they're sharing nostalgic memories. People generally get a 'Warm Glow' inside when relating to events and occasions in the past and enjoy reminiscences about how things used to be – even when these events sometimes have a painful side. When people speak wistfully of the past, they typically become more optimistic and inspired about the future.

We can all remember events surrounding friends and family, holidays, weddings, special occasions and nights out in Preston. So let your mind wander and think of the youthful days at the dance hall or courting in one of the many cinemas in the city. Be entertained as we take you on a sentimental journey through the pages of 'Memories of Preston'…. Happy Memories!

TEXT   TONY LAX, ANDREW MITCHELL, STEVE AINSWORTH

PHOTOGRAPH RESEARCH   TONY LAX

DESIGNER   SEAMUS MOLLOY

BUSINESS DEVELOPMENT MANAGER   PETER HOWARD

VICTORIAN & EDWARDIAN PRESTON

Below: Early Edwardian Preston was a fashion lifetime away from what we might see today. In those days, ladies went out to do their shopping dressed like the ladies they purported to be. Fine hats, ground length dresses and carefully chosen accessories marked them out as people of elegance and breeding. The building in the background is the former Farmers Arms Hotel, later renamed The Jolly Farmer. Here, we are looking at the scene on market day. There would later be a canopy erected over the open stalls as this area evolved into the fish market.

Right: A charming view of life at the turn of the last century, is taken at the premises of Harrison Brothers butchers, Victoria Road, Fulwood. This property, originally built as a house c.1851, was one of the first in the new freehold estate. It was converted to a butcher's shop c.1900. The property has since turned full circle and is a residence once more. The shop front is still there, complete in almost every detail; only the sign has gone, and the central door has been filled in to make a large bay window

Below: This is an interesting image from New Street and Market Place in the 1880s. The photograph shows the North side of Market Place with the entrance to Friargate to the left and New Street on the right. London Hat Warehouse can just be seen on the left with the shops on either side in the process of demolition. This row was later completely demolished to eliminate the narrow throat at the top of Friargate, and to allow for a better view of the Harris library. As a point of reference, today, the Cenotaph is centered about 20 yards down on the left side of New Street on the site of the old Swan Inn. The arched entrance to Pedders Court is seen to the right of the sign 'W. Poole'.

The Triumphal Arch on Fishergate was erected in 1885 to mark the visit of Albert Edward, Prince of Wales. The future king spent two days in mid July here, attending a meeting of the Royal Agricultural Society, meeting up with various leaders in the textile trade and laying the foundation stone of the Albert Edward Dock. The arch was a representation of Caernarvon Castle and was put up over the former tramway tunnel that went under here. Beattie's photographic studio and cheese merchants Livesey and Toulmin flanked the model. Both these buildings were swept away in the subsequent widening scheme that took place along the western edge of the station c.1910. This area would later be occupied by the Victoria Buildings on the north side of Fishergate and the Queens Buildings on the south side.

Top and above: This very old row was demolished in 1896 to make way for the Miller Arcade. Most of the town's butchers could be found displaying their wares behind the columns. The end property was Cottam's Shoulder of Mutton Inn, appropriately named given what was going on further down the road. At the other end of this row along The Shambles, towards Church Street, was a small building which was Prestons first Post Office. The property was demolished to make way for the Harris Library and Museum and subsequently the Miller Arcade. 'Shambles' was a name originally used for a street of butchers shops where meat was slaughtered and sold. It is derived from the Middle English word schamel, which meant a bench, as for displaying meat for sale. In the second old photograph, the open-top tram trundles towards the junction of Lancaster Road and Church Street, more commonly known today as Starkie's Corner. We can get a visual image from this photograph of how the rebuilding modelled this end of Lancaster Road after the Old Shambles was demolished, with the Miller Arcade and Harris Museum on the left.

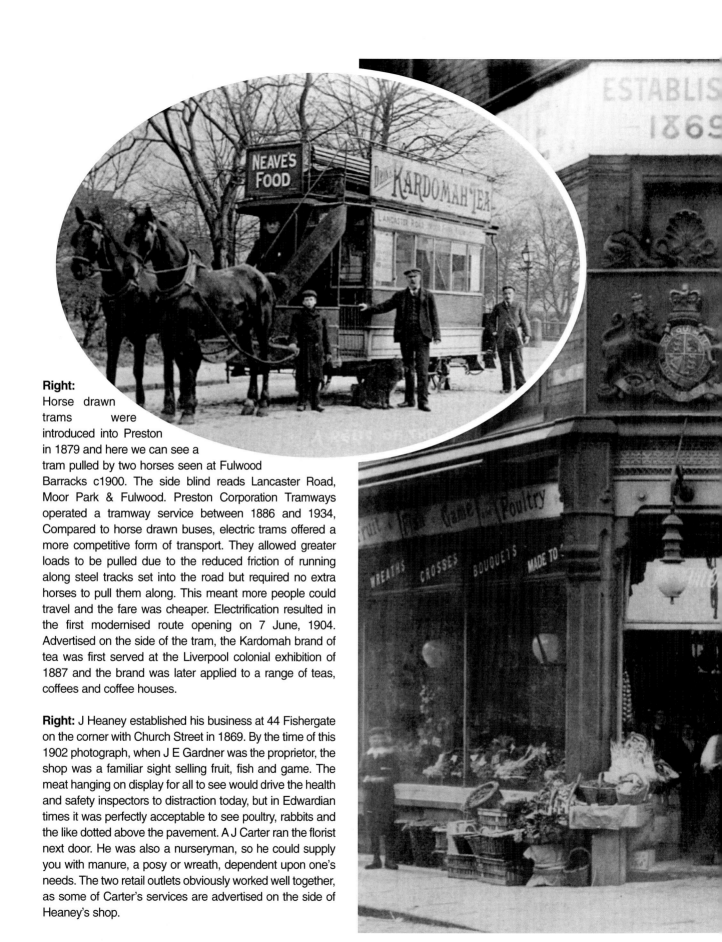

Right: Horse drawn trams were introduced into Preston in 1879 and here we can see a tram pulled by two horses seen at Fulwood Barracks c1900. The side blind reads Lancaster Road, Moor Park & Fulwood. Preston Corporation Tramways operated a tramway service between 1886 and 1934, Compared to horse drawn buses, electric trams offered a more competitive form of transport. They allowed greater loads to be pulled due to the reduced friction of running along steel tracks set into the road but required no extra horses to pull them along. This meant more people could travel and the fare was cheaper. Electrification resulted in the first modernised route opening on 7 June, 1904. Advertised on the side of the tram, the Kardomah brand of tea was first served at the Liverpool colonial exhibition of 1887 and the brand was later applied to a range of teas, coffees and coffee houses.

Right: J Heaney established his business at 44 Fishergate on the corner with Church Street in 1869. By the time of this 1902 photograph, when J E Gardner was the proprietor, the shop was a familiar sight selling fruit, fish and game. The meat hanging on display for all to see would drive the health and safety inspectors to distraction today, but in Edwardian times it was perfectly acceptable to see poultry, rabbits and the like dotted above the pavement. A J Carter ran the florist next door. He was also a nurseryman, so he could supply you with manure, a posy or wreath, dependent upon one's needs. The two retail outlets obviously worked well together, as some of Carter's services are advertised on the side of Heaney's shop.

Above: The cutting of the first sod for the Albert Dock took place in October, 1884, and in July the following year the first stone was laid by His Royal Highness the Prince of Wales, afterwards King Edward VII. In his honour the dock was called the 'Albert Edward'. During his two day visit HRH attended the annual meeting of the Royal Agricultural Society of England, which was held on Moor Park, and attended a gathering of cotton operatives in the Public Hall, where he was presented with specimens of cloth manufactured in the town. On the 17 July he laid the foundation stone of the Albert Edward Dock, having first attended a lunch in the Town Hall with the Mayor, Alderman John Forshaw.

Left: A rare photograph of Swansea Terrace, Watery Lane and the Grand Junction Hotel, decorated for the visit of the Prince Albert, the Duke of Edinburgh, in 1892. The view is looking west at the time of the opening of Preston Dock. On the right is the Grand Junction Hotel. The archway over the road carries the message, "Welcome Sailor Prince", probably referring to the Duke's service in the Royal Navy. The Dock was officially opened on 25 June, 1892.

Above: There can be no doubt who the star of the show is in this photograph from the Preston Guild in 1902. The large model of a pig is aboard the float of Richard Myerscough, wholesale provision merchant and sausage manufacturer, as they travel along Ribbleton Lane passing the junction with Barton Street, on 3 September, 1902. The Guild was an organisation of traders, craftsmen and merchants who had a monopoly of trade in the town. Only members of the Guild could carry out a craft or business and newcomers could only trade with permission from the Guild. The rarity of the event, and the fact that large numbers of people congregated in Preston for the occasion, made the Guild a special opportunity for feasting, processions and great social gatherings. The first eye-witness account of the Guild dates from 1682. There have been 26 Guilds for which records survive, held every 20 years - apart from a wartime interruption, which led to no Guild in 1942.

ENTERTAINMENT, LEISURE & PASTIMES

Right and below: How lovely it is to be able to get away from the hustle and bustle of city streets and spend an hour or two in one of those idyllic havens of ours, the public park. They are oases of calm in a desert of stress. A view of greenery and pretty flowers linked with the gentle noise of the waters are sights and sounds to soothe the most fevered of breasts. Miller Park is just south of the railway station, close to the Ribble. It was designed by Edward Milner on land donated by cotton industrialist Alderman Thomas Miller. As an English Heritage listed park, it has a number of impressive structures, including a sundial, grotto and fountain. The latter has interesting representations of earth, fire, water and air at its base. The fine statue depicts the Earl of Derby who was British prime minister when the park opened in 1867. Visitors are also taken with the beautiful Rose Garden, handsome bedding displays and the regal Derby Walk. The former Park Hotel, built in 1882, is now used as offices by the County Council. The accompanying photograph shows Queen's Park in 1928 with a neat little boathouse from where pleasure craft could be taken out for half an hour or so. Then, came the fateful cry of, 'Come in number six, your time is up'.

Below: Josh Macrae's 1962 song 'Messing About on the River' immediately comes to mind when you look at the photograph. Crowds of men, women and children in their Sunday best mess about in boats on the River Ribble. The embankment is as busy as the water so clearly these Prestonians were enjoying a boom in leisure time when this photograph was taken in 1929. The children are being given a very special Easter Monday treat with a boat ride on the River Ribble. At one time, boating on the river was very popular and lots of people enjoyed an afternoon relaxing on the water. You can just make out that temporary scaffolding is in place on the East Lancashire Railway bridge, possibly in connection with the replacement of the cast iron arch bridge spans. These were replaced with steel girders in 1930.

© LEP

Above: The little ones of reception class age cuddled their favourite china dolls. It was 1918 when the class at St Thomas's, on Lancaster Road, posed for the camera. The lad on the front row does not look too happy that he has to clasp the same sort of toy that the girls had. Back then, lads did not even play with the equivalent of an Action Man. It was all guns and cricket bats for them. The school ma'am looks to have been a stern lady. No doubt she imposed discipline with a firm hand. How many of the youngsters in her charge would have had no fathers to go home to, having lost them on the battlefields of Europe?

Above: St Ignatius' RC Primary is an inner city school situated close to the centre, just off the A6 North Road. Built in 1863, it had just celebrated its golden jubilee in the year before this photograph of the boys in Standard IV was taken. All-in-one desks and seating made sure that these lads sat fairly still in their places, with fidgeting kept to a minimum. The boys look a well turned out lot, sitting under the watchful gaze of Mr Hosker, the headmaster, on the left at the rear, accompanied by Miss C Roonie and Mr J Lacy. The school is still thriving and underwent refurbishment in 2000.

The mean streets of Preston. This photo looks much older than it is. You would be forgiven for thinking that it was taken in the 19th century but it actually dates from 1932. These are the cellared dwellings on the north side of Kirkham Street, looking towards Fylde Road. The properties were demolished in 1939. Today, by comparison, you would be looking at the very modern looking University of Lancashire Computing and Technology building.

All the fun of the fair, at the annual City Centre Whitsuntide Fun Fair in 1948. Thrill rides, children's rides, candy floss, toffee apples, hook a duck, ping pong balls in goldfish bowls and much much more are on offer every year at the traditional Flag Market location. The former Whitsuntide Fair dates back to the early years of the 19th Century, when it was held on the land known as The Orchard before the covered market was erected. People would come from all over Lancashire to buy and sell at a Preston fair. For hundreds of years the fairground was the domain of the actor and the jester, the magician and the minstrel, the puppeteer and the fire eater, the juggler and the tumbler. No Whitsuntide Fair would have seemed complete without Sedgwick's Zoo, Professor Anderton's Magic Show or Hughes' Boxing Booth. If you lasted three rounds with one of Bert Hughes' fighters then you got 10 shillings. After the Second World War crowds came flocking back to the fairground, where peep shows were as popular as the roundabouts. The fat lady, the thin man, the sword swallower, the tattooed woman and the ever popular India Rubber Man all added to the fascination and excitement of the occasion.

Centre: A fortnight of fun and festivities would not be complete without lots of dancing. This was certainly acknowledged to be the case in 1952, so the organisers of the Preston Guild earmarked £1,100 especially for marquee dances. A dance was held in Miller Park just about every night, in addition to a series of more formal events at the Public Hall. Our photograph was taken at one of the marquee dances in Miller Park, and judging from the stance of the dancers we think the band is playing a waltz. Following the success of BBC's Strictly Come Dancing, ballroom dancing has enjoyed a popular revival in recent years. All the glitz, sequins and camp glamour of the waltz, cha-cha and quick-step on the big screen, has encouraged many of us to give it a go! Until the arrival of the hit TV programme, ballroom dancing seemed destined to be the preserve of perma-tanned couples with fixed grins and gaudy attire dancing in competitions.

Thanks to Brucey & Co, however, the masses are getting involved in this exhilarating and pleasurable pastime like never before.

Bottom: It almost makes you shiver just looking at this photograph, as you know fron experience the water would have been freezing cold. These brave souls are taking advantage of the outdoor facilities at Waverley Park, open-air swimming baths, Ribbleton, Preston, in 1958. Such centres, also referred to as lidos, were very popular between the wars and continued to hold their position as premier league recreation well into the 1950s. Health and safety was not much of an issue, as children chased each other round and dived in from the concrete edges surrounding the pool. This was the place to be for any budding Johnny Weissmuller or Esther Williams of the time. The facility closed on more than one occasion in the 70s, but the plug was pulled for the very last time in 1979.

© LEP

Right: The original Theatre Royal, Preston, was built on the corner of Theatre Street and Fishergate in 1802 to cater for the large crowds expected for the Guild of that year. It seems that the Theatre Royal had a number of rebuilds during its history which lasted for 153 years. The first films were shown there in 1911, and it finally closed as a theatre for stage performances in 1928. It was remodelled as a cinema, reopening in June 1928 under the ownership of Associated British Cinemas (ABC) showing H. B. Warner in the film 'Sorrell and Son'. The auditorium now sat 1,160 people. It continued as a cinema until 3 December, 1955, when it closed, and was finally demolished in 1956, in order to build a new ABC cinema on the site.

Above: There are not many bars that you would get an enthusiastic welcome, as this one in Preston in 1953. How many bar staff do you see today that are so happy to please, with bright eyes, shiny black hair and a wet nose. Jet the dog looks like an old hand behind the bar, when it comes pouring drinks for his favourite customers. He was a very clever dog but hand pulled beer was a bit beyond him. The name of the pub where Jet worked was not listed but hopefully it would have been somewhere appropriate like, the 'Old Dog' or the 'Dog and Partridge', or even perhaps the 'Dog and Duck'.

Right: Located on Church Street at the corner of Tithebarn Street, the Empire Theatre opened 22 May, 1911, as a 2,500 seat variety theatre and music hall. It was the last theatres in Preston to convert full-time to film. The theatre closed in August, 1927, and re-opened as the New Empire three years later after redecoration and improvements had been carried out. It screened its last film, "The Last Frontier" starring Victor Mature, in 1964. In August of that year, actress Pat Phoenix (Elsie Tanner of Coronation Street) opened the Empire Bingo Club, which was operated by the Star Cinemas circuit. It closed in 1974 and the building stood empty for two years, before being demolished. Retail outlets were built on the site.

The roadsign says 'No Entry' to the one way Earl Street in this extremely busy market scene from c1960. The Victorian Covered Market is a Grade II listed landmark structure built 1870-75. The market consists of cast iron pillars and lattice work iron roof structure supporting a wood and glass roof. Major alterations were made in 1958 when the glass skylights were removed, electric lighting installed and the cobbled floor replaced. The much simpler and smaller structure opposite, the old fish market, was covered in 1924. Looking along Earl Street towards Lancaster Road, at the very end on the right we can just make out the old Police Station building. In the distance a solo Mark I Mini makes it way along the one-way street. The original economy car made by British Motor Corporation from 1959 was considered a British icon of the 1960s.

Above: Knitting is a skill that is not exclusive to women. In fact, in medieval times it was almost a largely male occupation and a knitting trade guild was started in Paris in 1527. Sailors were keen needle users as the necessary equipment was very portable and was a useful pastime in whiling away the hours on a long voyage. These lads, from the late 1940s, were casting on as part of a practical lesson in the grounds of the Harris Orphanage in Fulwood. The organisation was founded when the lawyer, Edward Harris, bequeathed a huge sum to be used for various cultural and philanthropic purposes. A village homes style of orphanage, along the lines of Dr Barnardo's in London, was built in the 1880s. The orphanage became a primary school in the 1950s, before relocating to Wychnor, and the old buildings were taken over by the Polytechnic.

Left and above: Were you in the crowd of exited fans as Beatlemania hit Preston? It was lucky Friday the 13 September, 1963, for these young fans as they struggle to watch their idols on stage at the town's Public Hall. This was The Beatles' second and final concert in Preston and formed part of their UK Summer Tour, which ended two nights later at the Royal Albert Hall, in London. They had performed in the Public Hall on one previous occasion, on 26 October, 1962. This, however, was the year it all really started to happen for The Beatles. After topping the chart with 'Please Please Me' the group never looked back. The 'Fab Four' can be seen on stage, well at least three of them, as they sing from a classic setlist that would have included songs like, 'From Me To You', 'She Loves You' and 'Twist and Shout'. After the show, Paul McCartney drove to the Imperial Ballroom in Nelson to be part of the judging panel for the Imperial Miss 1963 contest.

STREET SCENES AROUND PRESTON

A lonely tram makes its way down the middle of Church Street in this scene from Edwardian Preston. The overhead cabling had not long been in place and was still a novelty to the general public. Electricity was one of the marvels of the age. There was a lot of change and innovation for us to take on board about this time. The first wave of motor cars appeared on our roads and we even heard about some brothers over in Kitty Hawk, North Carolina, who were trying to develop a flying machine. Church Street is still with us, but Guy's Row to the right is now part of a new residential area. Further down, the Albion Saw Mills and Walker's chemist's belong to the past, as does Briggs opposite. But the Lamb Hotel, on the left, is still there after all this time.

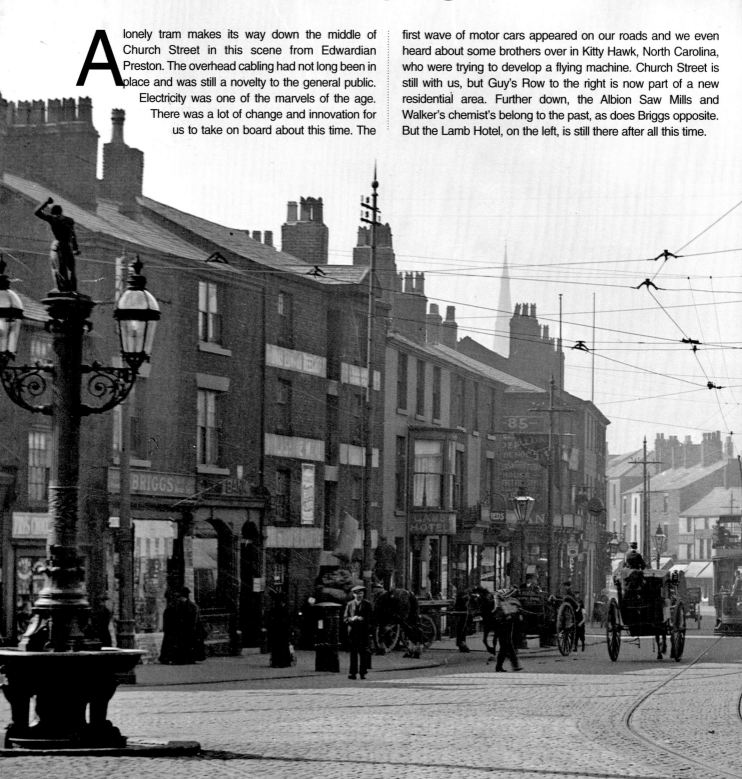

Left and bottom left: In the street scene from just before the First World War, the poster on Dickinson's barber's shop on Friargate advertised a show at the Empire. This theatre opened as a 2,500-seat music hall in 1911. The acts being promoted on the poster included the Griffiths Brothers, a slapstick act, Bert Erroll, a top female impersonator, and Lillie Soutter. Her rendition of 'Red Wing' was one of the hits of the era, popular with soldiers at the front. The companion Friargate view, captured just a few years earlier, shows a busy street scene with a tram outside the Hippodrome Theatre. Designed by J J Alley, it opened in January 1905. Charles Coburn, famous for his 'The man who broke the bank at Monte Carlo', was first on stage. It was regarded as a very safe theatre, having numerous exits, a modern iron safety curtain and up-to-date fire hydrants. The word 'Royal' was added to its name in the 1940s, but that did not save it from closure in 1957. It was demolished two years later.

Above and below: This view, showing the junction of Church Street and Lancaster Road, is looked upon as the centre of town, and shows a tram approaching Starkie's corner. The handsome buildings on the left of the photograph occupy the site of the old "Shambles" which were erected in 1715, and is now the site of the Miller Arcade. Church Street has existed since medieval times, but Lancaster Road was not laid out until the Victorian era. Electrification resulted in the first modernised route opening on 7 June, 1904. Preston had an extensive street tram system, which like those in almost every other town in Britain, was removed when buses began domination of local public transport. The Starkies name has been preserved in Starkie's Chambers, although the retail business has now gone and is today an outlet of 'Richer Sounds'. The Leather Shop next door was established in 1917 and at one point traded from the Starkies building.

This is a rare and typical street scene from the 1930s. On the far left of the image is the portico of the Empire Theatre and Empire Billiard Hall. Just a bit further along Church Street, is yet another portico, that of the Palladium Theatre whose marquee advertises 'Laughing Sinners' with Clark Gable. 'Laughing Sinners' was a 1931 Metro-Goldwyn-Mayer feature film also starring Joan Crawford as the leading lady. Just protruding above the roof of the tram car is a control signal, one of two on this very busy section of track. The other was situated at the bottom of Grimshaw street and controlled access inbound towards the town. Just beyond the leading edge of the tram is the junction of Tithebarn Street.

Left The chimneys belonged to the William Calvert's Flats Mill. At the start of the 20th century there were 3,000 cotton looms here. The site was razed in the 1980s to make way for the Capitol Centre. Coming over the Ribble at Walton Bridge, Fishwick in 1938, the cars were passing Shawe's Arms and heading for Preston from Walton-le-Dale. Formerly the Black Horse until 1843, this London Road pub still sits here alongside a road that is now a busy dual carriageway. The Belisha crossing, fairly new in the picture and long before zebra style markings were thought of, has been replaced with a central refuge, helping those wanting to get safely into Ashworth Grove on the right. A cycleway goes behind the pub today.

Bottom left: Cars line the street in this late 1950s view looking west at the shops on the south side of Fishergate. Businesses seen either side of the entrance to Cannon Street are: Dolcis Shoes, T. Mears, H Samuel advertising Everite Watches, The Mitre Hotel, Owen Owen and British Home Stores. Restricted access and double yellow lines prevent any sort of parking on this section of the street today.

Below: A reminder of the past is this photograph of Cheapside, Market Place from 1960 with the Maypole Butter Store and Boots on the right. Next to the Maypole is the low roofed building, that includes a tobacconist, behind the Bedford van, next to Kettering & Leicester and Weaver to Weaver. This building is believed to be Preston's oldest shop, with distinctive Dickensian windows and a genuine slice of old England that contrasts sharply with its neighbours. The present shop was once the home of the Town Surgeon Dr. Wortton. He was recorded as occupying the property in 1684. During a renovation of the old shop in the mid 1980's it was found that the supporting timber frame was numbered so that it could easily be assembled on site.

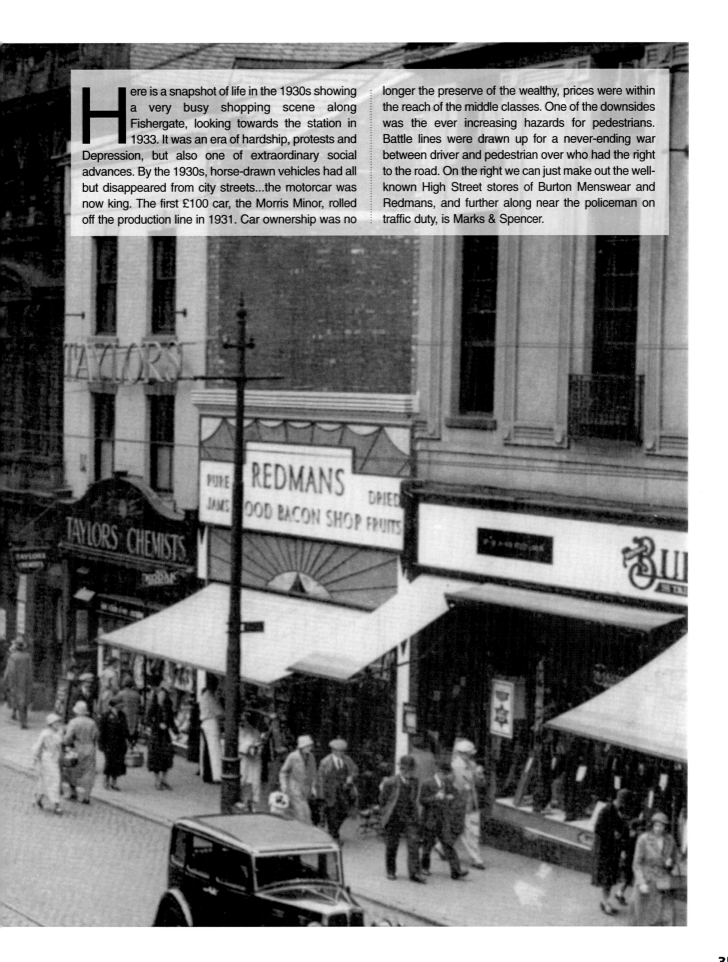

Here is a snapshot of life in the 1930s showing a very busy shopping scene along Fishergate, looking towards the station in 1933. It was an era of hardship, protests and Depression, but also one of extraordinary social advances. By the 1930s, horse-drawn vehicles had all but disappeared from city streets...the motorcar was now king. The first £100 car, the Morris Minor, rolled off the production line in 1931. Car ownership was no longer the preserve of the wealthy, prices were within the reach of the middle classes. One of the downsides was the ever increasing hazards for pedestrians. Battle lines were drawn up for a never-ending war between driver and pedestrian over who had the right to the road. On the right we can just make out the well-known High Street stores of Burton Menswear and Redmans, and further along near the policeman on traffic duty, is Marks & Spencer.

In medieval times, Preston was a small community situated above the flood plain of the river, handily placed at the foot of the Pennines at the lowest fordable spot and limit of the tidal flow up the Ribble. By the time of the Hundred Years' War, there were some 2,000 inhabitants hereabouts. Most were within a stone's throw of what is now the Fishergate part of town, seen here at various times from late Edwardian times to the end of the 1950s. Preston may have been the centre of the region, but its catchment area was poor. Although the burgesses added more buildings in the area, it was not until the textile industry began to blossom from the late 17th century onwards that the town began to show elements of prosperity. However, it would be in the following century that the industrial revolution truly took hold. By the time we reach the era reflected in the oldest of these images (left), the town centre had begun to take on the sort of shape that would serve it well for much of the 20th century. Motor cars appeared on the streets that had already had their surfaces cut by tramlines. When we move on to the scene from just before the last (bottom left) war we can see that Fishergate has got busier still. There are some household names about which we can reminisce. Did you buy a pair of shoes at Saxone, seen on the left, or stop for a cuppa at the Kardomah close by? Perhaps you went to the pick 'n' mix counter or bought a cheap LP at Woolworth's across the road. Post-war Fishergate is captured above and below, who is old enough to recall the bobby on point duty on Church Street at the intersection of Glovers Court and Fishergate?

It is really interesting to compare these two photographs looking along Deepdale Road, over 50 years apart. The pictures were taken from infront of HMP Preston, with the County Arms Hotel prominent to the right-hand side of shot. Visiting judges to the Assize Courts are believed to have stayed at the hotel. In the earlier atmospheric picture (below) we can see the tramlines and evidence that horses have been on the cobbled road, but no motorised vehicles. In the main image from 1955, large crowds had gathered at the junction of Deepdale Road and Ribbleton Lane to catch a glimpse of the Queen and Prince Phillip. The pilot vehicle was leading the royal cavalcade through Deepdale during the Royal tour of Lancashire. Since the demolition of the County Arms, it is amazing how the entire character of the area has changed.

A less common view of the old Town Hall from 1957, looking down Cheapside from Fishergate. After fire struck on the night of 15 March, 1947, it was decided by the Town Council to demolish the building, but this was directly against the wishes of the public who had put together an eight thousand signature petition to have it saved and restored to its former glory. However, this never happened and the lower part of the building was stabilised and used for various purposes until 1962 when it was completely demolished to make way for the new and modern Crystal House. The pedestrians seem oblivious to the line of traffic waiting to exit the one way street. In the distance we can just make out the old Post Office building behind the trees.

Left: A fabulously atmospheric photograph taken along Friargate, some time shortly after the opening of the Royal Hippodrome Theatre in 1905. We can see from the protruding wall clock on the building adjacent to Kays at 158 Friargate, that it is 1.25pm. Handcarts and bicycles were the order of the day, although evidence that a horse trams ran along the street, can be seen between the tramlines. In the misty distance, we can see the purpose built building to house the Public Library and Museum. Building work officially started on the museum in 1882 during the Preston Guild and it officially opened in 1893. People lived and worked on Friargate. The street also welcomed travellers and market-goers. In the past, those in search of entertainment could visit the Hippodrome theatre to take in a show. Today Friargate is still a main thoroughfare into Preston and centre for nightlife, although this view is dramatically different.

Bottom left: One of the last photographs to show this area of Friargate in its original form, looking towards Market Place in 1962. Only a few years later the properties on both sides of the street would be demolished to make way for the new Ring Road development. Familiar names such as Cavendish Furniture, Brighter Homes, Harrops and Ellwalds Fabrics would be lost to the developer. The Morris Minor would no longer be able to access Friargate from Lune Street, as this is now an attractive looking pedestrian precinct. From the opening in 1966, the right-hand side of the picture would be taken up by The Mall, more recently St George's Shopping Centre. The Harris Library and the tip of Preston Parish Church steeple are visible in the background.

Below: Nile Street was situated just off the north side of Church Street, almost opposite Manchester Road. The decorative feature above the doorways seen on the left was very common in the town and became known as 'Preston ears'. On the right is the Anchor Inn, one of the Dutton's houses on the corner of Nile Street and Church Row. The residents of this peaceful street had come out in force to see what the cameraman was up to in this scene from 1956. Nile Street and other terraced street in this area, were about to come under the spotlight as part of the second big wave of compulsory purchase and demolition.The Council had estimated that there were still approximately 5,000 people in Preston living in inadequate and overcrowded conditions and needed rehousing.

BUILDINGS & MONUMENTS

There was not much activity in the square, so we have to think that this was not a market day. The stalls seem largely deserted, with just a handful of people dotted around the scene that is dominated by the Town Hall. Over to the left, the Crown Hotel was one of four inns that fronted Church Street. This was where the Arndale (Miller) Arcade would later be created and a new Crown incorporated into it. There are some names on the shops to the right that are period pieces. Smith Brothers were hatters in the days when men more toppers, derbies, bowlers and homburgs. Coward Brothers ran the grocery store next door, with the Maypole just beyond. Founded in Wolverhampton in 1887 by George Watson, this was one of a chain of what became 1,000 dairies across England. On the corner, footwear was available at Butler's.

Right: A picture of the entrance to Fulwood Barracks which was built in 1848. The characteristic sandstone was quarried at Longridge and brought by railway to Fulwood, with the first stone being laid in August 1843. According to the Queens Lancashire Regiment Museum website it is the most complete example of mid-Victorian military architecture in the country. Fulwood Barracks was the last and largest of a chain of barracks built in the North West in the wake of the Chartist riots of the 1830s. The barracks has throughout its history been the main focus of military activity in the County, often with much wider responsibilities. It has been the home of the Queen's Lancashire Regiment, and other regiments, and is now the site of the Queen's Lancashire Regiment Museum.

Bottom: The foundation stone of the present handsome Harris Institute building, on Avenham Lane, was laid in June, 1846, by the then mayor, the late Thomas German, esq. The building was officially opened in October, 1849. The approach, or entrance terrace is in the Italian villa style, and was designed by Mr. George Latham. The Preston Institutuion for the Diffusion of Useful Knowledge, or as it was popularly known, "The Mechanics Institute" moved into the building at the end of Avenham Walk in 1850. In 1882 the trustees of the late Edmund Robert Harris, a local solicitor who had died in 1877, endowed the Institution. A number of houses in Regent Street were purchased and demolished so that the Institute could be extended. The Institute, henceforth to be known as the Harris Institute became a centre of excellence for the teaching of Art and Science. .

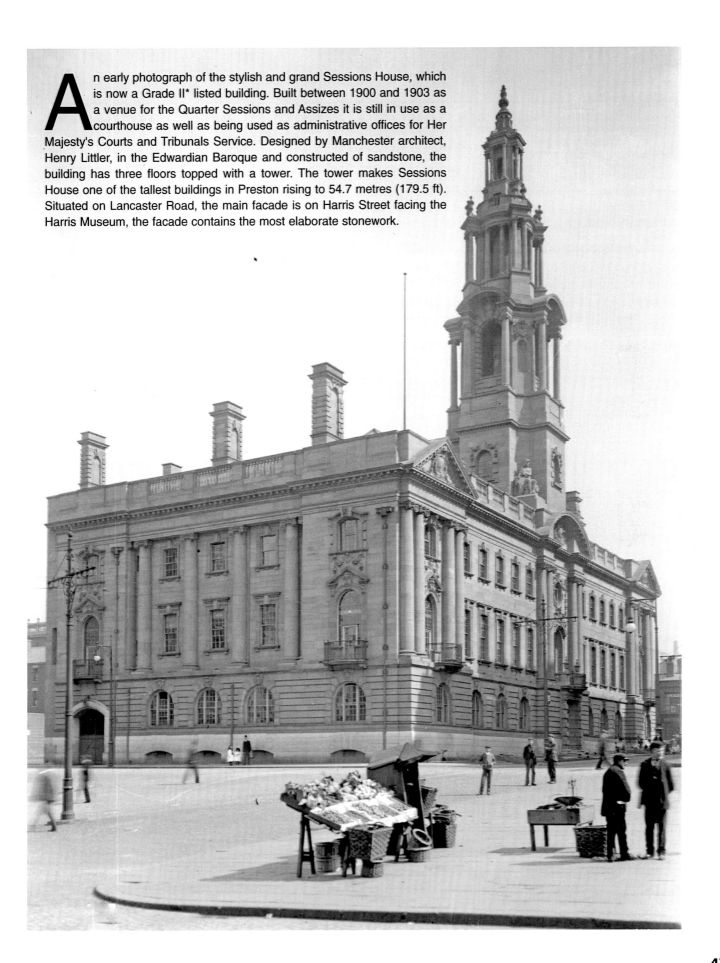

An early photograph of the stylish and grand Sessions House, which is now a Grade II* listed building. Built between 1900 and 1903 as a venue for the Quarter Sessions and Assizes it is still in use as a courthouse as well as being used as administrative offices for Her Majesty's Courts and Tribunals Service. Designed by Manchester architect, Henry Littler, in the Edwardian Baroque and constructed of sandstone, the building has three floors topped with a tower. The tower makes Sessions House one of the tallest buildings in Preston rising to 54.7 metres (179.5 ft). Situated on Lancaster Road, the main facade is on Harris Street facing the Harris Museum, the facade contains the most elaborate stonework.

Below: Preston's Corn Exchange (Public Hall) has changed shape a number of times during its long and varied existence. It is recorded that the market here opened on 26 August, 1824. The building was constructed in a Georgian style and consisted of a number of large rooms around an open court covered by a glass roof. It served as corn exchange, meat market and cloth market, and contained small shops, but as time passed it was used less and less for trade. Following extensions it was no longer oblong, and canopies were added as seen on this photograph. In 1842, at the height of protests for the right of the vote for men, a demonstration took place outside the Corn Exchange and cotton workers who were protesting were fired upon by the military resulting in four deaths. A statue of the Preston Martyrs by Gordon Young was unveiled outside the Corn Exchange in the late 1980s to mark this event. The building was remodelled as the Public Hall in 1881-82 and a hall and gallery were added for meetings and entertainment. In its new format the building could accommodate 3,300 people. As Preston's smartest meeting and entertainment complex it hosted performances by artists such as The Beatles and Rolling Stones in the early 60s and you could get a 'Whole Lotta Love' from Led Zepplin in 1971. It was the place to be until its closure in 1972, after which it lay unused. The demolition of the main body of the building was fiercely opposed, and it was not removed until the early 1990s. The Grade II listed building began life in the 21st century as a public house known as the Flax and Firkin, which more recently became The Assembly and has become part of the nightlife of modern Preston.

Above: The delightful view across the lawns towards the Royal Infirmary dates from the early 1900s. The little group sitting patiently on the bench was perhaps waiting for someone to emerge and give a display of tennis to entertain them. As with most places, Preston was a dirty, unsanitary town in the early 1800s. As well as the usual diseases and ailments, local inhabitants suffered two cholera outbreaks in 1832 and 1848. Even deep into the Victorian age, many townspeople still used earth closets. At least it eventually had an Infirmary to help ease major medical problems. Deepdale Hall was built in 1833 and was turned into this ahospital in 1870. Situated at Stanleyfield Close, off Deepdale Road and not far from the football stadium, terraced housing now blocks the view of this fine edifice. The Infirmary closed in 1987 and became a hall of residence.

Right: Preston Grammar School was a fine educational establishment, both architecturally and in the learning that it provided.

With links back to the 15th century, the school took its place on the corner of Cross Street and Guildhall Street, just off Winckley Square, in 1841. It had been designed and built by John Welch, a local stonemason. This 1957 photograph shows the old building being demolished. By then, it had become the home base of the engineering section of the GPO telephone service. The school had long relocated to Moor Park Avenue, making that its home just before the First World War.

in 1872. Flooding caused severe problems to parts of the Tram Bridge tressle support structure and by 1965 the timber bridge was much decayed. It was replaced by a modern concrete bridge designed to look as much like the original as possible. It survives in a recognisable form and parts of the road itself can be walked today.

Below Market Place is the historic core of the town that only became a city in 2002, thus truly living up to its description as 'Proud' Preston. This area has been the focus of major events

Above: The Old Tram Bridge, viewed from the south bank of the river towards Avenham Park. When this bridge was new in 1802 it was still called 'old'. The engineer for the tramway was the celebrated Benjamin Outram and the tramway system became known as the Outram Way. The tramway linked to the bridge via a large incline at Preston (steps and a footpath through the park mark its former location). After the bridge, the horse-drawn tram continued along a 1.1km tree-lined embankment to Penwortham Mill, before rising to Walton Summit on another incline. Tramway operations ceased around 1860 and ownership of the bridge was given to the Preston Corporation by the London & North Western Railway

for some 800 years. It also contains some of our most important and finest buildings in the Harris Museum, Sessions House, Town Hall and former Head Post Office. The impressive cenotaph was unveiled in 1926, somewhat later than comparable memorials erected in other places to respect those who had made the ultimate sacrifice in the 1914-18 War. Designed by the eminent architect Sir Giles Gilbert Scott, it was paid for by public subscription. There is a Roll of Honour, also designed by Scott, in the Harris Museum on the staircases that face the main door. After the Second World War, the Cenotaph was rededicated to all who fell in the protection of their native land.

Right: Firefighting for much of the 19th century was largely given over to bodies of men recruited by insurance companies or those community spirited people who volunteered their services. Preston's Fire Brigade established a fire station on Tithe Barn Street in 1852, in the shadow of where such a structure once stood. It was rebuilt in 1900 and extended five years later when three bays were added. The appliances photographed date from c1937. In 1961 the fire service then moved to new premises on Blackpool Road. This area was cleared in 1963 to make way for the bus station.

was a modern building with seating provided in stalls and circle levels. After a fall in popularity, the ABC was closed in April 1973 to allow for a Painted Wagon pub to be constructed in the rear stalls area. It re-opened on 6 May, 1973, using 637 seats in the circle area only. It was eventually closed in September 1982, and demolished four years later.

Above and right: The hoarding advertises Preston's latest luxury cinema, during the construction of the ABC on 15 September, 1958. The ABC Cinema was located on the corner of Fishergate and Theatre Street on the original site of the Theatre Royal, which had opened in 1802. The new cinema opened to the public on 14 March, 1959, with Rex Harrison in "The Reluctant Debutante". Film star Richard Todd appeared in person on the opening night. The cinema

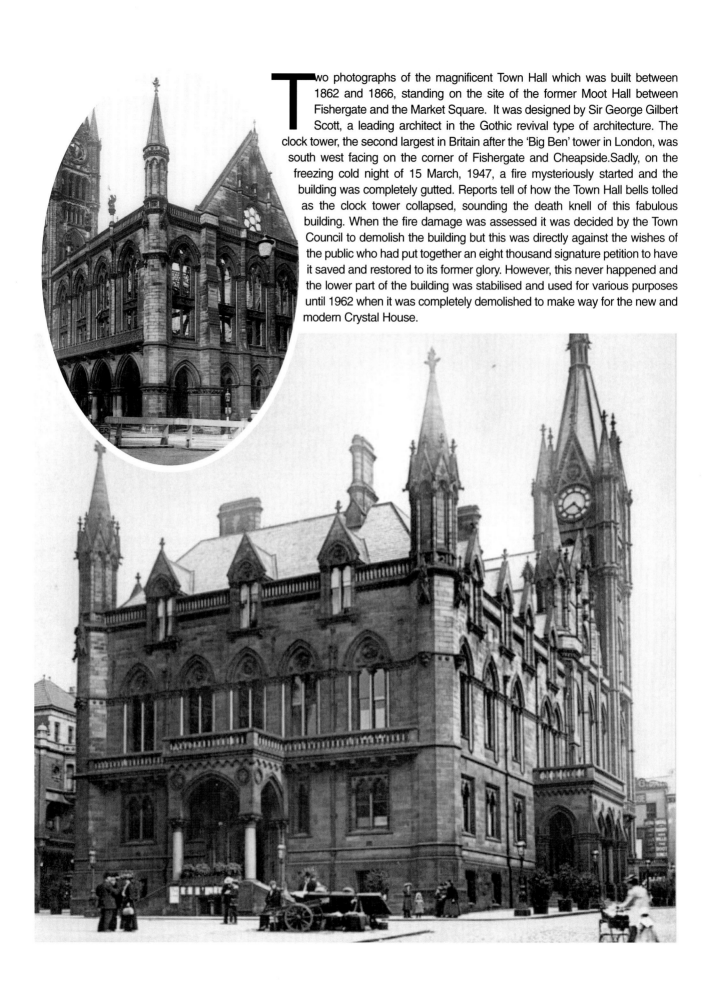

Two photographs of the magnificent Town Hall which was built between 1862 and 1866, standing on the site of the former Moot Hall between Fishergate and the Market Square. It was designed by Sir George Gilbert Scott, a leading architect in the Gothic revival type of architecture. The clock tower, the second largest in Britain after the 'Big Ben' tower in London, was south west facing on the corner of Fishergate and Cheapside. Sadly, on the freezing cold night of 15 March, 1947, a fire mysteriously started and the building was completely gutted. Reports tell of how the Town Hall bells tolled as the clock tower collapsed, sounding the death knell of this fabulous building. When the fire damage was assessed it was decided by the Town Council to demolish the building but this was directly against the wishes of the public who had put together an eight thousand signature petition to have it saved and restored to its former glory. However, this never happened and the lower part of the building was stabilised and used for various purposes until 1962 when it was completely demolished to make way for the new and modern Crystal House.

Right: The site of the Parish Church has been used as a religious building for several centuries. Originally, the ancient church of St Wilfrid occupied the site, only to be rebuilt and renamed In the 16th century.St John's Minster, formerly the Church of St John the Evangelist, is in Church Street, in the centre of Preston. The site of the Parish Church has been used as a religious building for several centuries. Originally, the ancient church of St Wilfrid occupied the site, only to be rebuilt and renamed in the 16th century. In 1581 its dedication was changed to Saint John the Baptist. It was repaired during the following century, but by 1770 its condition had deteriorated. In that year its dedication was changed again, this time to Saint John the Evangelist. In 1811 the tower was partly demolished, to be replaced by new tower in 1814. However by 1853 the church was in such a bad condition that, apart from the base of the tower, the whole church was demolished. The new church, designed by E H Shellard, was built between 1853-1855. The gates to the churchyard and the gates are listed at Grade II.

Below: The North Road Wesleyan Chapel, now known as City Church Preston, is about the only recognisable feature in this photograph from 1949. Walker Street is a now a narrow one-way road to the left of the church. The traffic lights have gone and you certainly wouldn't consider strolling across the busy North Road dual carriageway today. The unusual underground toilets have been removed, as has Park Lane Mill seen at upper right. The public toilets had ironwork similar to those opposite the Miller Arcade in Church Street.

Above: St Matthew's Mission Church looks much the same today as it did way back in the mists of time, early in the last century. The young believers belonged to a religious community who first met in the building on Acregate Lane in 1887. The Mission, along with St Matthew's Church and that of St James, are now part of the Parish of the Risen Lord. The style of service is Bible based and includes songs of worship. When established, the chapel here served a catchment area of terraced housing that was home to workers at the many cotton mills in the locality.

Right and facing page: The Preston Cenotaph in Market Square, presents an interesting contrast to the Post Office building seen immediately behind. The Post Office was opened in 1903 and when this image was taken had endured years of the town's sooty atmosphere. The Cenotaph is a monument to soldiers from Preston who perished in World War I and II. Unveiled on 13 June, 1926, the memorial was designed by Sir

Giles Gilbert Scott with sculptural work by Henry Alfred Pegram. Scott, who was architect of the classic British red telephone box, Liverpool Anglican Cathedral and Tate Modern, described his design as conforming to the 'Greek feeling' of the square. The entire monument is 70ft (21m) tall and is in Portland stone. The monument's main feature is a figure of "Victory" whose arms are raised and who holds laurel wreaths in either hand. At the very top of the monument there is an empty coffin (hence "cenotaph" or "empty tomb") with cherubs and strands of foliage carved around it. The names of those honoured are contained in a Roll of Honour located in the nearby Harris Museum. This Roll of Honour is inscribed on marble tablets on the ground floor of the building. The names of some 1,956 Prestonians are thus recorded.

The names of all 1.7 million servicemen and women of the Commonwealth forces who died during both the First and Second World Wars are commemorated on the Commonwealth War Graves Commission website.

Above: On 8 July, 1913, every vantage point was occupied when King George V and Queen Mary paid us a visit. Decorated trams, festooned with flowers and messages of support and loyalty to the royal couple, brought traffic to a halt on Lancaster Street and neighbouring thoroughfares as the entourage entered Market Square. The motorcade arrived at the Town Hall steps and the King and his consort emerged to be met by Mayor William J Hayhurst and accompanying VIPs. Included in the party was Edward Stanley, 17th Earl of Derby. Three years later, he would become Secretary of State for War. The cheers of the crowd could be heard in Fulwood and down at Bamber Bridge. It had only been just over two years since the Coronation and this was, for nearly everybody, a first opportunity to see the monarch and his wife in the flesh. The band of the 4th Battalion of the Loyal North Lancashire Regiment struck up a welcoming march and a huge choir of 800 schoolchildren sang a specially composed song, 'Queen Mary'. George and Mary lunched at the Bull and Royal Hotel, visited the Horrocks and Crewdson mill on Stanley Street and later went on to Kirkham, Lytham St Annes and Blackpool.

Right: Soon after the start of the First World War, Earl Kitchener, the War Minister, encouraged local councils to set up groups of volunteer recruits. These were drawn from sets of friends, neighbours and workmates and became known as 'Pals' Battalions'. It was thought that this would improve fighting spirit as comrades would support one another better than strangers. Preston was no different to other towns and men signed up in large numbers, many viewing the situation as a jolly adventure that would be 'over by Christmas'. The reality would be starkly different. On 7 September, 1914, these Pals met in Market Place before a patriotic and supportive crowd before setting off to training camps. Eventually, they would see service at Loos, the Somme and in Flanders, many did not return

EVENTS & OCCASIONS

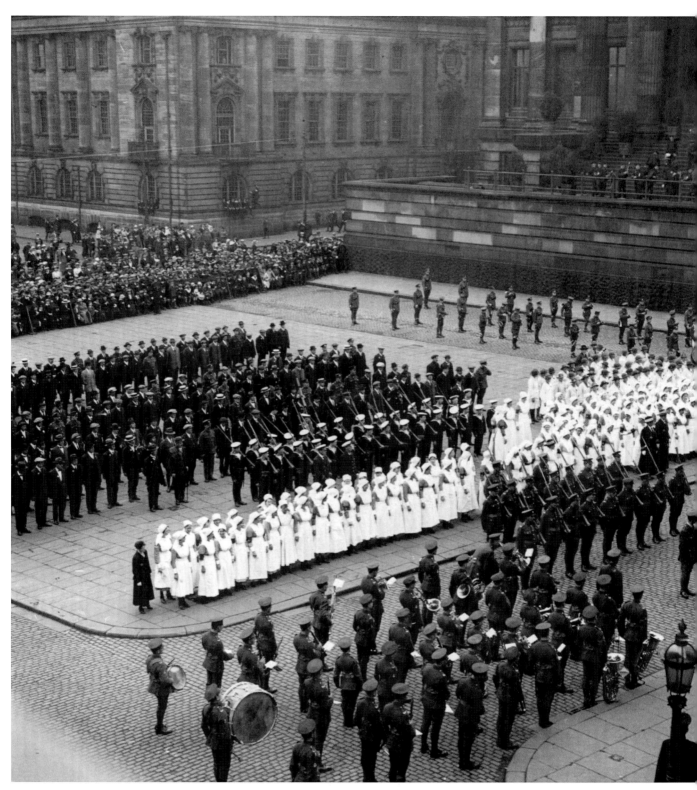

Above: Although fighting in the First World War ended on 11 November, 1918, it took some time for all combatants to make their way back home from some of the furthest outposts of the theatre of conflict. This Peace Day parade was not held in the Market Place until 19 July, 1919. Many of those on parade were, by then, ex-servicemen, but that did not matter. Participants and onlookers alike were just glad that it was all over and that they could start rebuilding their lives. Officially, the war did not end just because bombs and bullets were not flying through the air any more. Negotiations to agree the Treaty of Versailles continued long into 1919 as the Germans struggled to hang onto what they could and the victors turned the screw in the matter of reparation demands.

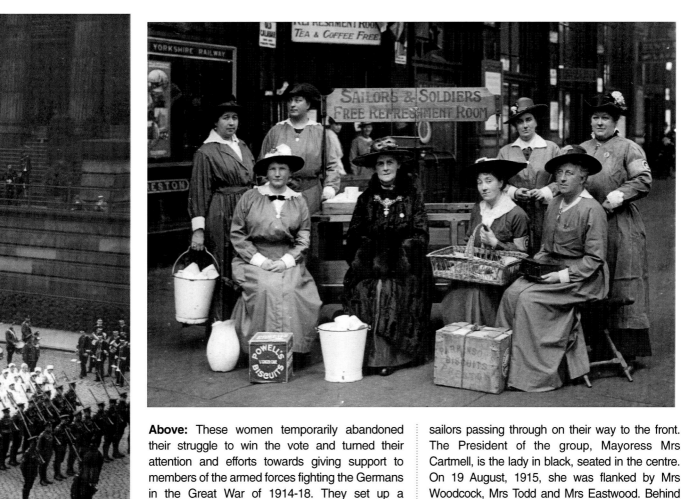

Above: These women temporarily abandoned their struggle to win the vote and turned their attention and efforts towards giving support to members of the armed forces fighting the Germans in the Great War of 1914-18. They set up a committee to run a buffet at Preston Station for soldiers and sailors passing through on their way to the front. The President of the group, Mayoress Mrs Cartmell, is the lady in black, seated in the centre. On 19 August, 1915, she was flanked by Mrs Woodcock, Mrs Todd and Mrs Eastwood. Behind them were Mrs Blackhurst, Mrs Bell, Mrs Foster and Mrs Threlfall. Anyone in uniform received free refreshments. Some of the volunteer women put in 12 hours at a time, 'doing their bit' for the war effort.

Left: Many people seem to think that women taking over traditional male roles on the factory floor, behind the wheels of lorries or bringing in the harvest from the fields was something that happened in the last war. The so-called fairer sex rolled up its sleeves in the First World War, manufacturing ordnance in munitions factories, driving ambulances and, literally, bringing home the bacon. These young women were on a recruitment drive when they brought their tractor and plough along Garstang Road and onto North Road. They were members of a procession that hoped to raise awareness and attract volunteers to swell the ranks of the Women's Land Army. A recruitment poster of the time said, 'God speed the plough and the woman who drives it'.

The Children's Pageant was a significant part of the 1922 Guild celebrations and this display shows that just about everyone had made a special effort. St Ignatius' School had been given the brief of adopting costume suitable for the early Stuart period in English history. 'Merrie England' was the theme and merry was the mood here.

Elsewhere, school groups put on musical and dramatic shows, including a truly memorable 'Midsummer Night's Dream'. Children had real fun and that was what is was all about.

Avenham Park was packed with performers and onlookers all enjoying themselves with gay abandon. Maypole dancers, troupes of jesters and Elizabethans being punished in the pillory all had their parts to play. There had been a torchlight procession and parade of

floats through the streets, something first seen in 1882 and a practice continued ever since. The focus of the original 1179 market was close to the entrance of the present Miller Arcade in the city centre. The earliest Guild roll, a list of merchants that still survives, dates from 200 years later. By then, the tradition of holding a major event had not only become established, but prospered. The 20-year cycle was formalised in 1542, but, by the 18th century, things had become somewhat old hat and the occasion threatened to disappear from the calendar. Happily, it was re-structured as a first rate social occasion, becoming a celebration of the town and its people. Some famous stars of the entertainment world were featured as special attractions in the 19th century, including the Niagara Falls tightrope walker, Blondin. He came to Preston in 1862. Now, it is an occasion of civic pride, sending out a positive message about our town the length and breadth of the land. Even the phrase 'once in a Preston Guild' has become commonplace in our language.

The oldest of these church processions (above) possibly dates from 1902. In early Victorian times, the Catholic population in Preston grew significantly and a number of places of worship were founded, such as St Ignatius', St Augustine's, St Walburge's and St Joseph's. The little girls in their white outfits, clutching pretty posies of flowers, were on Moor Lane. They were parishioners of English Martyrs, the RC Church founded as a small chapel at Gallows Hill in 1865 until a large church could replace it two years later. Behind them was the funeral cortège for Canon Taylor, a leading figure in the history of this church. The other photograph is linked to Guild celebrations from 1922. In the picture the Church of England parade had reached the Red Lion and appears to be heading back on itself.

The bunting and banners festooned Lune Street as the nation got together to share in the Coronation celebrations. Neighbourhoods adopted the sort of patriotic fervour that had not been seen since the end of the Great War. After months of unrest, rumour and argument towards the end of the previous year, at last the abdication crisis that surrounded the royal family was done and dusted. Edward VIII gave in to pressures of which he had been the architect and went off with his lover and future wife, Wallis Simpson. His brother inherited the role of monarch and, on 12 May, 1937, we welcomed George VI to the throne. Although he was the reluctant king, never wanting the limelight, his consort, the former Elizabeth Bowes-Lyon, played a significant role in bringing a much needed stability to Buckingham Palace. Elsewhere in the town, dignitaries paraded formally and took part in official ceremonies in and around the council offices. Church services were held and many fine speeches made. The majority of the members of the ruling classes breathed a sigh of relief that anarchy had been avoided and they were happy to see the former king out of the way. By the time of the Coronation, most Britons had wearied of the ins and outs of the abdication saga. Most ordinary folk were happy to celebrate the event in the way they knew best, by having a party. Coincidentally, the Coronation took place on the day originally earmarked for Edward to receive the crown.

Above: Leaving the creation of a permanent acknowledgement of the sacrifice made by those who fell in the war until the summer of 1926 was not popular with those who had served in the conflict or lost loved ones on foreign fields or under the seas. Most other places had managed to raise a memorial before Preston. At least, when we did no-one could deny that the Cenotaph was a handsome and fitting tribute. The sculptural work was carried out by Henry A Pegram. It contains a central figure of 'Victory', arms held aloft holding laurel wreaths in either hand. There is an empty coffin at the very top, with cherubs and strips of foliage carved around it. Every year we pay homage to those gallant men and women, 'Lest we forget'.

Right: Belgian children found sanctuary in Preston during World War II. Pictured on 21 July, 1944, at Flag Market, infront of a brick air raid shelter. Nearly 300 youngsters, along with some teachers, spent most of the war years in local schools. The Trinity Catholic School alone accommodated almost half of

these pupils. When the refugees went home in 1946, they presented the people of our town with a handsome, bound book full of memories, souvenir photographs, details of activities and a list of the names of all those who gained shelter from the Nazi occupiers of their country. The front cover showed the flags of both of our nations and was a wonderful memento for the town to keep.

An inspection of Preston's First World War veterans by King George VI and Queen Elizabeth was in progress in front of the Town Hall, when this photograph was taken on 17 May, 1938. This was the second contact the royals had with the people of Preston within the space of a couple of weeks. King George VI was at Wembley to see Preston win the FA Cup Final 1-0 on 30 April, and he presented the trophy to winning captain Tom Smith in front of thousands of cheering Preston fans. In this photograph, we can only imagine how proud these gallant old soldiers must have felt to gain the approval of the King and Queen. A large crowd turned out, and shop workers left their counters to see the popular Royal couple perform the ceremony in the Market Square. After leaving the County Hall, the King and Queen were driven to Moor Park to inspect 2,500 members of the British Legion. War was once more looming on the horizon and King George and Queen Elizabeth and their two beautiful daughters lived and suffered with the people of Britain through the dark days that followed.

© LEP

Top left: Goalmouth action from the 1938 FA Cup final between Preston North End and Huddersfield Town. This was a historic and momentous occasion in football broadcasting, as it was the first to be televised live by the BBC. The game, however, failed to live up to its billing, which prompted a comment from Lieutenant-Commander Thomas Woodrooffe, a former naval officer who had become one of BBC radio's top broadcasters, that he would live to regret. At 0-0 the game went into extra time, and by the 120th minute he announced to the viewing nation that "if there is a goal now, I'll eat my hat". Moments later George Mutch was brought down in the Huddersfield box and after he had dusted himself down, he just about managed to get the ball past Bob Hesford in the Huddersfield goal for a 1-0 victory. A dramatic finish to a dreary game, with the prospect of Woodrooffe eating his bowler hat still to come.

Left and above: Cheering crowds waiting for the commencement of the victory parade at the entrance to Preston Station on 2 May, 1938. Two days earlier Preston had lifted the FA Cup against Huddersfield. The celebrations were even greater as Preston had been losing finalists the previous year. An army of policemen try to guide the open-top single decker buses along a packed Fishergate, as the team arrive home to a heroes welcome. Every vantage point is taken and we can see people are even hanging out of the upstairs windows of E J Reed & Sons, Peter Hayes Florists and the Theatre Hotel. Players, including captain Tom Smith, goalscorer George Mutch and little known Bill Shankly, are enjoying the cheers from the adorning fans as they proudly show off the newly acquired trophy. The Leyland Motors coaches, operated by Scout Motors, carried the team on to a victory parade at Deepdale and then on to a Civic Reception.

Above: Some older Prestonians will no doubt remember the occasion when this atmospheric photograph of a demonstration of air raid precautions was taken in 1938. War was looking inevitable, and for the first time in history aircraft were capable of carrying bombs over long distances, so the citizens of Britain faced a very real threat from the air. On 15 March, 1938, a meeting was held in the Guild Hall in Preston, followed by demonstrations of emergency procedures in the market place. Young and old learned how best to protect themselves and their families in the event of an air raid. In World War One mustard gas had been used with deadly effect by Germany, and it was widely expected that they would employ the use of gas again. The picture shows two rubber-suited workers who would be expected to deal with any major attack. A young boy, photographed by a press photographer for posterity, helps out with the demonstration. From the look of it he might not be able to sit down for a while!

Below: After nearly six years of conflict, the end was in sight. With Hitler dead in his bunker, the Germans had thrown in the towel. The national mood was one of rejoicing and, during early May 1945, street parties, parades, fine oratory and simple merrymaking were all part of the way in which we let off steam. This formal procession made its way past the Town Hall on 13 May, just under a week after we had heard the good news that the war in Europe was at an end. Although many of the brave members of our armed forces were still making their way back to Blighty, locals turned out in force to show their appreciation of those in uniform marching past. Of course, there were still the Japanese to be dealt with, but our American allies would finish off that task.

Left: This photograph was taken on 7 March, 1945, and another Royal Visit encourages the loyal citizens of Preston to hang on for just a while longer. Huge crowds had turned out to welcome King George VI and Queen Elizabeth (later the Queen Mother). Their Majesties went on to chat to wounded soldiers outside the Town Hall. Both the King and his Queen stayed in London during the Blitz and survived the bombing of Buckingham Palace, taking tours out to the devastated areas of the city to show solidarity with their people. Though the town fared better than many during the war, each person had his or her story to tell, some of personal tragedy, many of amazing fortitude in hard times. But the light at the end of Britain's long dark tunnel was growing brighter. Two months after this visit of the King and Queen to Preston, Adolf Hitler committed suicide in his Berlin bunker. On 7 May, 1945, Germany surrendered unconditionally, bringing the war in Europe to an end.

Flags and bunting are stretched across Allen Street from window to window as part of celebrations to mark the end of hostilities in 1945. Looking south-west towards the junction with Adelphi Street, neighbours and friends line up for the photograph. The entire community around Allen Street went wild with joy when the news that everyone had been hoping for was announced. Patriotic flags floated gently in the breeze and 'Welcome Home' notices were made to greet the returning troops. It was good to be alive and, along with the rest of Britain, they found the energy to let their hair down and organise a knees-up after six long years of war.

Victory celebrations held after the defeat of Nazi Germany and Japan in World War II. The official WW2 'Victory Celebration' took place on 8 June, 1946, for what was believed to have been a "People's War" - the Allied Armed Forces supported by all the civilian groups. Rationing was still in place, but special dispensation was given by the Minister of Food so that children and the elderly could partake of a public tea as part of the day's celebration. Here are two really cute pictures from Avenham Park on the day. The children are enjoying the free milk, but what is still noticeable is the lack of adult males.

© LEP

We celebrated VE and VJ Days in the summer of 1945 and showed off our loyalty to our new monarch in June 1953 on the day of her coronation. A street party is the way in which we Brits like to enjoy such occasions. In Preston, though, we had the chance for an extra in September 1952. This was not the end of a war or the start of an era we toasted, but the latest Preston Guild. We should have had fetes and festivities in 1942 as part of the 20-year cycle, but we had other things to deal with across the Channel, in the Far East and North Africa. The families on Floyer Street made up for missing out 10 years earlier and had a jolly time. Bunting was stretched over the street and every doorway was decorated with bowers and garlands.

Centre After a break of 30 years, because of the war, Church Street again became a riot of coloured pennants and flags for Guild celebrations, with its lamp standards spiralled in two colours like maypoles. During the course of the festivities, many a happy parade wended its merry way along Church Street, which was part of the processional route. Here we see the Women's Class from the Parish Church putting their best feet forward, watched by a tremendous crowd. As well as all the traditional processions, the programme of festivities on that occasion included a Veteran Car Rally, an amusement fair in Miller Park, the Industrial Exhibition at Moore Park and numerous other exhibitions throughout Preston, as well as sports, schools events, dancing, and much more. As usual the grand finale was a torchlight procession through the streets, culminating in a firework display in Avenham Park, and at midnight the National Anthem was played by massed bands in Market Square. The Ritz cinema, seen on the right, showed a special film entitled 'Proud Preston'.

Bottom: On a thankfully warm and sunny day, proud parents and grandparents were among the hundreds of admiring spectators who crowded into Avenham Park to watch the Guild Festival for Schools in 1952. The subject of this particular display has long been forgotten except perhaps by a handful of adults who took part in the Festival long ago when they were children. We can gather from this atmospheric photograph, however, that groups of young boys dressed in extravagant and colourful costumes proudly played their part for their mums and dads, while just for the day 70 or so little girls were fairies, all dressed in white with gauzy wings spread, and performed their dance in an almost perfect circle. Perhaps they are all Sugar Plum Fairies from 'The Nutcracker' ballet. The Preston Guild Merchant has often been referred to as 'England's greatest carnival.' Be that as it may, the celebrations brought together the town's schools, churches, industries, and sporting and hobbies enthusiasts in a way that nothing else could.

having a fantastic if rather chilly time as their vehicle passes the Old Black Bull public house (whose proprietor, by strange coincidence, was W.A. Watt.) James Watt, whose premises were situated in Paley Road, were importers of timber, sawmillers and casemakers, and specialised in Neptune domestic woodwear. Their floats each carried examples of finished and partly finished joinery work. The Trades Procession at the Preston Guild Merchant of 1952 was held on Wednesday, 3 September, and the spectators along the route are obviously taking no chances with the vagaries of the British weather!

Below: A Preston Corporation Public Baths float in the Preston Guild procession of 1952. From the look of it, not everyone is happy about the situation. Maybe playing the roles of movie stars, Esther Williams and Johnny Weissmuller was not all it was cracked up to be on the back of a float driving round Preston streets for

Above: The Preston public gain every vantage point, including the first floor windows of 'Rose for Gowns' bridal outfitters, to watch the Trades Procession of 1952. The rather windswept girls on one of James Watt's tableaux are

several hours. Preston Corporation Baths, on Saul Street, were open all year round for swimming, slipper baths and remedial baths. There were also open-air pools at Haslam, Moor and Ribbleton Parks.

© LEP

This party at Brownedge Road, Lostock Hall, near Preston, was just like thousands of similar events, held the length and breadth of the country on or around 2 June, 1953. It was a celebration to mark the day when Queen Elizabeth II was crowned in Westminster Abbey. The weather was overcast, but this did not dilute the enthusiasm for a good party. Trestle tables and benches were borrowed and mums slaved away all day making lots of goodies, including fairy cakes and potted meat sandwiches. Joyful scenes, rivaling those witnessed on VE Day, took place in every village. Children were dressed in their Sunday best to sample the delights put on the tablecloth in front of them. It was a special day, and those lucky enough to have a television set suddenly found themselves to be very popular. Neighbours crowded into their front room to watch the ceremonies being relayed from the capital.

A great action shot of one of English football's greatest and most gifted players, Tom Finney, during a match towards the end of his career in 1959. Sadly, at the time of writing, the ledgendary footballer had just passed away at the age of 91. He was born on a street near the Deepdale stadium in 1922 and spent his entire 14-year career with his home-town club. Finney made his debut for Preston in August 1946 and soon established himself as an agile forward. Post-war demand for plumbers ensured that he had a second income to supplement the £14 he received as a footballer and was nicknamed "The Preston Plumber". During his incredible and modest career, he wore their famous white strip 433 times and scored 187 league goals. Despite his on-field success he was a down to earth character and so, win, lose or draw after the game he'd meet his wife Elsie and they'd get the bus home together. Only when forced out with a persistent groin injury in 1960, did he retire from Preston North End. On 27 February, 2014, thousands of people lined the streets to honour Sir Tom Finney as his funeral took place at Preston Minster. In attendance were big names from the football world, including David Moyes, the Manchester United manager, and Sir Bobby Charlton, who both managed Preston. The funeral service was full of respect and tributes to a true football legend.

© LEP

number of years about the crime ridden state of Lancashire it was decided in 1839 that a combined county force was required to police the county. In the same year, the force was founded and Captain John Woodford was made chief constable with two assistant chief constables, 14 superintendents and 660 constables. By 1965, the force had an establishment of 3,784 officers, making it the second largest police force (after the Metropolitan Police) and the largest county force in Great Britain.

Below: Stanley Carwin opened a shop on Corporation Street in 1922, selling radios or 'wirelesses' as they were often known back then. Obviously a far sighted individual, he is said to have been the first person to import a radio set from the newly established Phillips' factory in Holland. It was about the time that he went into business that the BBC started

Above: The boys in blue stand to attention as they are presented to HM Queen Elizabeth during a two day Royal Visit to the county in 1955. The young and elegant Queen Elizabeth was only three years into her reign when she visited the Lancashire Constabulary H.Q. at Hutton in April 1955. She was accompanied by the tall and youthful looking Duke of Edinburgh, who is not in this shot. After many complaints over a

broadcasting from Station 2LO, at Marconi House, in London. In later years, Carwin's would have outlets on Miller Arcade and Fishergate. In 1960, the company mounted a display as part of the Trades' Exhibition in the Public Hall. By then, the company had branched out into retailing various other electrical goods that included Murphy TVs, Dansette record players, Frigidaire fridges and Thor washing machines.

TIME GENTLEMEN PLEASE!

There are few institutions so central to Britain's community life as the local pub. The pub is often the centre or hub of the community and can also provide essential services beyond the usual drinks, food or entertainment. With the closure of so many local shops, churches and even schools, the pub is often the only truly local meeting place left. Yet despite this, Britain is currently estimated to be losing around 20 pubs a week. In the Preston area we have lost more than our fair share of colourful old pubs over the years. The following few pages give a small selection of these hostelieries that have been lost to us since the Victorian era. Just how many pubs, inns and beerhouses there were in Preston over the last two centuries is not clear, but one man, namely Steve Halliwell, has made a fantastic effort to record the relevant information. We would thoroughly recommend you have a look at his unique website (http://pubsinpreston.blogspot.co.uk/) to discover the fascinating stories and inrtigue surrounding the pubs and inns that once stood proudly on your local streets.

SHOULDER OF MUTTON, MOLINEUX SQUARE

The introduction picture above right shows the Shoulder of Mutton back in the 1880s when William Cottam was the proprietor. The 'Shoulder' was situated on the Old Shambles, which ran between Church Street and Market Street which is now classed as Lancaster Road. The pub would have opened in the late 18th century and after approximately one hundred years of trading succumbed to progress and was demolished. Where it stood is now the site of the Harris Free Library and Museum.

LEA'S VIRGINS INN, ANCHOR WEIND

This old Virgin's Inn, formerly the Curriers Arms, was the last thatched tavern in Preston. The ancient building is said to have once been a farmhouse, and in its later years was used by country women who had come to market, and could get cups of tea. This photograph was probably taken around 1890 just before its closure, when the Lea family ran the Inn. Thomas Lea is recorded as Mine Host in 1873 and Jane Lea is listed as the publican in the 1881 and 1891 census details. It was demolished in 1894 as part of the town improvements. Anchor Weind was a short street off Friargate, near the junction with Market Street, and the Inn would have been situated at the side of what today is the former Post Office. Directly behind the Inn, to the right of the large chimney, is the new Harris Library building, which was under construction and opened in 1893. In front of the Harris Library would be the market stalls on the Flag Market.

THE BLUE ANCHOR – BLUE ANCHOR COURT

A rare photograph of the Blue Anchor Inn which was on the east side of the Market Place on the site now occupied by the Harris Library. This photograph was taken c1883 when most of the surrounding properties had been demolished to make way for the Harris Museum, Art Gallery and Library. The inn along with the other properties had been part of a compulsory purchase order in September 1883. The men are standing in Blue Anchor Court, which was only a few feet wide before the demolition of the whole of the east side of Market Place. The Court entrance is immediately below the anchor. The Blue Anchor Inn was on the right hand side of the Court (see below).

THE CRAVEN HEIFER AT THE JUNCTION OF PARK ROAD AND NORTH ROAD

This well known public house stood on the corner of Park Road and North Road. The last landlord before the property was demolished in 1936 was former Preston North End player Tommy Roberts. The rear of the premises was also the location of Charles Green's balloon ascent in 1828. The area has changed dramatically since this image was taken. Note the underground lavatories similar to the ones in front of the Miller Arcade.

THE CASTLE HOTEL, CHEAPSIDE

A photograph of the Castle Hotel from around 1906. Originally known as the Castle Inn, it was built in 1623. A favourite watering hole and meeting place for many Prestonians, the Castle Hotel was situated in Cheapside opposite the Market Square, almost directly opposite the Harris Museum and Art Gallery. Around 1910 the Castle Hotel was purchased by the Refuge Assurance Company, was transformed into commercial premises and was then known as 'Castle Chambers'. In the lower right of the image is the Argenta Meat Company based in Oldham who, interestingly, eventually became Dewhurst's The Master

Butchers. To the left of the butchers is the a narrow underpass that originally led to the courtyard behind the hotel which later became a thoroughfare leading to the premises of the Lancashire Evening Post. Their vans would use the passageway to collect newspapers from the presses for delivery. In the early 1990s, following the closure of Castle Chambers in 1989, the whole of the building was remodeled and was replaced by shops as it is today.

APOLLO INN, 45 (LATER 151) NORTH ROAD

The 1950s double-decker makes its way out of town past the Apollo Inn on the way to Holme Slack. The Lion Breweries Apollo Inn is a long gone watering hole that occupied the corner of North Road and Walker Street. The Craven Heifer was opposite, on what was a rather complicated junction of roads. It was the point where the present North Road split, with Park Road forking to the left and North Road continuing into the town centre. Just out of shot, further along the cobbled setts, was the underground urinals with the distinctive iron railings. It is believed that the Apollo was a favourite of popular comedian Tommy Trinder, on his occasional visits to Preston. As well as being a much loved entertainer, Trinder was also a die-hard Fulham F.C. supporter and became chairman in 1959. The Apollo was demolished c1965 to make way for the new ring road.

BOROUGH TAVERN AND GREY HORSE AND SEVEN STARS, FISHERGATE

These photographs show the frontage, on Fishergate, of the Borough Tavern alongside the Greyhorse and Seven Stars in 1923. By this time the latter had closed down, with the rear part of the inn to become part of the Lancashire Evening Post, after being purchased by George Toulmin. Opposite the top end of Cannon Street, the inn had a long history, dating back to the 18th century, when it was known as the 'White Horse and Seven Stars'. The Borough Tavern at 123a, Fishergate, is seen here above and behind the premises of Palatine Rubber Co. The tavern dates back to the 1850s, but prior to that it is believed that as far back as 1684 an inn known as the Holy Lamb was on

the site. This could explain why the Borough Tavern used a 'lamb' as an illustration on its sign. Like the Grey Horse, the Borough Tavern was also bought by the Toulmin family for extensions to the press room of the newspaper.

ROYAL HOTEL, 23 CHURCH STREET

Not to be confused with the Bull & Royal Hotel on the opposite side of Church Street. Over the years this hotel has been known by a number of names. Initially it began life as the Albion Hotel around 1832, later becoming the Imperial Hotel, and eventually the Royal Hotel. Links to riotous behaviour and seedy entertainment in the 19th century could be the reason behind the name changes in an attempt to blur the establishments poor reputation. The entrance to the right of the image led to the hotel yard. Off the hotel yard was an old warehouse that was at one time used as a 'low-class' concert hall in the 1840s, one of the earliest in Preston. This photograph was taken during Preston Guild Merchant celebrations in 1902, welcoming visitors to Preston. As we can see from the posters, on offer was beer on draught, Special Guild Cigars, John Dewars Whisky and Worthingtons bottled beers. The building was demolished in 1913 with and the Palladium Cinema built on the site two years later.

REGATTA INN, 59 FISHERGATE HILL

OLD LEGS OF MAN, 3 FISHERGATE,

This is a very interesting image looking across to Moore's Regatta Inn on Fishergate Hill. We can date the opening of the Regatta Inn to 1837, at which time a notice appeared in the Preston Chronicle, where an application was made by Mr Edward Gardner for a Messuage or Dwelling House at the bottom of Fishergate, to be used as a Retail Beer House called the Regatta Inn. The inn was demolished in 1914 to make way for the approach to the Penwortham New Bridge, over the Ribble. The bridge opened in 1915 and we can clearly see construction work being carried out in the background. Thomas Moore was the last landlord from 1904, hence the name on the signage. The view today is unrecognisable, as it is now a busy road junction and you would probably need to stand in the Chorley Nissan Garage on Strand Road to get a similar shot.

The Old Legs of Man was a well-known inn and was commonly referred to as "The Legs". It was situated directly opposite the (Old) Town Hall in Fishergate. The inn dates back to the early part of the 19th century and had a distinctive three legs sign on the front of the building. The landlord in 1821, Joseph Croft, was noted as a pioneer of bath chairs in Preston. This mode of transport became fashionable at this time and was the successor to the elegant sedan chair. In 1823, Croft became the landlord of the Red Lion. The photograph is from around 1910, when Frederick and Ellen Aston were the final keepers of the Inn. This could well be them posing outside in the coach entrance. The building was acquired by the County Bank and demolished in the 1930s, to be replaced by the bank building extensions. Today you may recognise the window on the right as that of Waterstone's Bookshop.

EAGLE AND CHILD, 139 CHURCH STREET

The Eagle and Child Hotel is thought to date back to the late 18th or early 19th century. The property was owned by the Earl of Derby until 1890/91. This was the most famous of the Derby Inns, and has a connection with Sir Thomas Lathom and Lathom House. It was situated between the Parish Church of St John to the left and the Preston Conservative Club and Discount Book Company, to the right. The Club was above the wonderful old bookstore which can be seen in these photographs. The small passageway between the church and the hotel was known as St. John's Place. After the Eagle and Child was demolished in 1937, the right of way became known as Stoneygate thus acting as an extension of the old street to the south east of the church.

HOOP AND CROWN, FRIARGATE

We can see in this photograph that unfortunately time has been called on the Hoop and Crown, in Friargate. A long history, dating back to the 1780s is about to end as the premises are already closed in preparation for demolition in 1938. Readers may not remember the Hoop and Crown but may recall the dance school that occupied the new Coronation Chambers building that replaced it. The wrought-iron canopy of the Royal Hippodrome can just be seen on the right edge of this picture. The Hippodrome continued to entertain people for another 20 years before it too had to make way for progress.

NEW COCK INN, NEW COCK YARD

The New Cock Inn could be found off Fishergate, and it is probably one of the oldest buildings in Preston as it was originally part of the domestic quarters of Winckley mansion. In 1795, part of the old house was demolished and the back section became the New Cock Inn. The inn gained a reputation for fine ale as far back as 1810, due in a large part to the the inn's first landlord, William Ashcroft. He was the first of several generations of the Ashcroft family who have served Preston well in their day. The cock as a symbol for inns dates from the Romans and may also have a religious significance. At one time, cock fighting was prevalent in the district and this is where the names of the inns like this may have been derived. The inn, together with the old passageway, has now gone completely, so this view of the yard from c1938 acts as a visual reminder.

ANGLER'S INN, POLE STREET

Matthew Brown was the Angler's' first landlord and lived here in the middle part of the 19th century, on the opposite side of the street to his famous brewery. He was listed as mine host from 1839–1859. The sign above the door of the Angler's Inn of a fisherman complete with fishing rod and net which extended over the pavement below, was unique among pub signs. His brewery was in Pole/Percy Street which is between the bus station and Church Street. In 1883 he had malthouses at Lark Hill, Maudland, Moor Park and Lawson Street and 46 pubs/beer licences. Old Tom was a speciality and was well known as a strong beer. It is believed the angler in the stonework pub sign was a good friend of Browns named Thomas Banks. It is not too much of a stretch to guess where the name 'Old Tom' may have been derived.

OLD SIR SIMON, FRIARGATE

The Old Sir Simon was situated on Friargate. The photo shows the pub decorated for the opening of Preston dock in 1892. This pub was named after Sir Simon Fraser, the 11th Lord Lovat. He was among the Highlanders defeated at the Battle of Culloden and convicted of treason against the Crown. The promise of a Dukedom secured Lovat's support during the last and most successful Jacobite uprising in 1745, when Bonnie Prince Charlie reached as far as Preston. The rebellion failed, however. After the defeat, Lovat one of the most colourful characters in Scottish history, was found hiding in a tree. He was the last person to be executed in the Tower of London, when he was beheaded there on 9 April, 1747. Opposite the Sun Hotel, which is on the corner of Great Shaw Street and Friargate, the premises today will be more recognisable as the left half of what was Bello's Restaurant and prior to that, the Torella Coffee Bar.

BARLEY MOW, NEW HALL LANE

This is the Barley Mow public house, 1, New Hall Lane, Preston, c1905. We are looking at the building from the Stanley Street end of the lane. It is believed to date back as far as the late 1830s, when James Whittle Snr was the host. Around the time this photograph was taken the proprietor of the Barley Mow Hotel was advertising Mathew Browns Prize Medal Ales, along with wines and spirits of the Finest Quality, in addition to a billiard table. The building may be more recognisable in recent times as a yacht chandler's. Across the road was the Rose Bud public house.

CORPORATION ARMS AND SPREAD EAGLE HOTEL, LUNE STREET

This image from 1960 is taken from directly in front of the Public Hall, looking towards the junction with Friargate. The Corporation Arms is on the left, and the old Spread Eagle Hotel on the right. Other than the front of the Public Hall, this part of Lune Street was swept away to accommodate the new Ring Way scheme in the mid-1960s.

The Corporation Arms building consisted of two wings around a triangular yard, with 21 rooms in all. Because of the extensive stabling it effectively became the "Corporation pound" for stray animals. The pub is perhaps more famous, however, for its links to the Chartist riots of 1842. As the name suggests, it was owned by the Town Corporation and its walls received a fair amount of shot during the conflict. Marks left by musket balls were still visible above the doorway prior to demolition.

The Old Spread Eagle Hotel was opened in 1802, when Lune Street was built, and it may have taken its licence from 'Matty's Whim', Chapel-walks, an inn that dated back to the 1700s. The old inn once stood nearby in the passage that led to St George's Church. Sadly, like the rest of the buildings in this 1958 photograph, the Old Spread Eagle would be lost to the developer just a few years later.

THE SIR WALTER SCOTT INN, 303 (LATER 24) NORTH ROAD

In August 1881, these premises served as the location of one of the town's most infamous murders, that of 16-year-old Annie Ratcliffe. Annie came to Preston with her parents from Darwen. On the morning of 3 August, Annie set out to marry John and left the Blue Bell Inn which was kept by her parents. On the way to St. Paul's Church, Annie met John Aspinall Simpson and they both went into the Sir Walter Scott. An altercation then took place wherupon Aspinall cut Annie's throat with a razor he had bought that morning. After doing the deed, Aspinall nonchalantly sat by and waited for the police to arrive. The subsequent trial found him guilty and he was hanged at Strangeways prison in Manchester on 23 November, 1881. This photograph of the pub was taken in 1958 just prior to demolition, in preparation for the new bus station.

FYLDE TAVERN, 213 CORPORATION STREET

This photograph from Preston town centre around 1960, shows the Fylde Tavern in the centre of a row of businesses on the Corporation Street roundabout. In the early days, the address would have been Friday Street, later to become Corporation Street. Friday Street was the short length of road in front of the main UCLAN Foster building, today called Adelphi Quarter. We know the Fylde Tavern dates back to 1839 because on this date, beer-shop keeper, Robert Latham was fined £12.10s for selling a glass of whisky to an excise man. Imagine how much that would be today. Older readers may also be able to make out antique dealers, Edward Nield and part of the Star Cinema, on the right of this picture. All these properties were due for demolition to make way for extensions to the Harris College (now the University of Central Lancashire).

DERBY ARMS, 36 LORD STREET

Two views of the Derby Arms on Lord Street, showing the front and back of the premises. The original pub was called the Joiners Arms and the new name was only acquired after the Derby Arms, Back Lane, closed down, around the turn of the last century. Both properties were owned by the Earl of Derby. The property next but one to the Derby Arms, as we look at the photograph, was the Green Man Inn. This part of Preston, was completely redeveloped around 1970, when it was earmarked as the site for the new Civic Hall.

standing in the doorway of the old Stanley Street Police Station and Preston jail. Only a few years after this picture was taken, the colourful lives of several generations of Preston families would be changed forever, as the demolition experts moved in to wipe away these buildings as part of the Ring Way Scheme.

KINGS ARMS, 31 STANLEY STREET

The Kings Arms was situated on the corner of Stanley Street and Church Street and probably dates back to 1837, when Edmund Gardner was Mine Host. The building is unrecognisable today compared to the attractive public house it once was in this photograph from c1955. It became The Kings Head around 1995, but this was short lived and it closed in the late 1990s. It had previously been called Joplins for about ten years. More recently the building has been used as a fast food outlet.

THEATRE HOTEL, 49 FISHERGATE

An external view of Boddingtons' Theatre Hotel and Commercial on the corner of Fishergate and Theatre Street, prior to its redevelopment. The original three-storey tavern dates back to the 18th century. Its proximity to the splendid Theatre Royal offered customers the opportunity to have a drink either before or after seeing their favourite artists of the time. From 1959 onwards, this would be cinema-goers after the demolition of the Theatre Royal to be replaced on the same site by the ABC. Only a year later, the hotel itself got a complete makeover. The building was completely modernised and reduced to a two storey structure, with a two-tone exterior. During the re-build the show went on, and locals had to stand in a temporary bar whilst building work went on around them. Trade continued until 1987 when the building was demolished.

THE HARP INN, CHURCH STEET

An interesting photograph of the Harp Inn, Church Street, from 1961. The building to the right of the Harp Inn was once a beerhouse called "Fortune of War", which was actually classed as being on Mill Bank. Former Preston footballer George Tod was the landlord of both, one after the other, between 1917 and 1924. From his debut in September 1900, Tod went on to make a noteworthy 140 appearances for Preston North End. The ginnel between the two buildings was known as 'Jerry Lobby', which led on to Edmund Street. At the time, the photographer could have been

PRESTON TRANSPORT

The Preston Corporation Tramways electric tram making its way along Broadgate, was one of the earlier models of closed top cars. It had an external staircase that led to the upper deck. Climbing up it was a draughty experience and could be dangerous in wet weather as the steps became slippery. More trams were built at the Dick, Kerr Works on Strand Road, than any other factory in Britain. Dick, Kerr were a Scottish electrical engineering company who moved to exploit the rapidly growing tram industry in the late 19th Century. Their tramcar business became part of English Electric and continued until the mid-30s, when most towns started moving to motor buses. Broadgate runs south alongside the Ribble from the bridge on the A59 Liverpool Road to the next bridge down, near Kilruderry Road, from where this photograph was probably taken.

Left and bottom left: The three buses parked on the cobbles must have been among the first ones that were acquired when Ribble Motor Services was founded in 1919. Its influence would spread all over the northwest, from Carlisle to the southernmost Lancashire borders. Its largely poppy red livery was distinctive and it served passengers well until taken over by the Stagecoach Group in 1988. With just a few exceptions, Ribble largely relied upon Leyland to supply its vehicles. Its head office was in Frenchwood Avenue, Preston, so we can truly claim that it was a local company. It had its roots in Motor Omnibus Proprietors, owned by J Hodson. His buses ran along a route from Gregson Lane, near Bamber Bridge. When Ribble took over this business, it had just a pair of wooden barns as its base, backed up by a stone-built workshop. The next generation of vehicles included the sleeker looking single deckers seen at the pick-up point outside the Sessions House and the Harris Museum. The former is a courthouse that dates back to the first few years of the last century. It is in daily use as a Crown Court. The imposing Harris Museum is also an art gallery and library. Its building costs were funded by the local lawyer E R Harris who bequeathed the then vast sum of £300,000 in his 1877 will.

Below: The gleaming new version 100E Ford Popular would be virtually straight off the production line in 1959. The Motor magazine tested a 100E in 1960 and found it to have a top speed of 69.9 mph (112.5 km/h), acceleration from 0–50 mph (80 km/h) in 19.6 seconds and a fuel consumption of 33.2 miles per imperial gallon. The test car cost £494, including taxes, with a comment that it was the lowest-priced orthodox saloon on the British market. This photograph from 1959 shows a section of the shopping parade along Langcliffe Road on the Brookfield Estate. Brookfield is a large estate of 530 homes, consisting of 1950s low rise flats, houses and bungalows. Behind the Ford Popular and the smartly dressed young lad on his trike, can be seen the shops of Norman Theobold, Southworths Bakers and Confectioners (also Post Office) and George Seymour. This busy little shopping area looks very similar today, overlooking a big grassy area. Although the shop names have changed, the look and feel is still very traditional.

A great shot of a variety of different vehicles from the 40s and 50s, viewed looking east towards Garstang Road. This stretch of the road between Brook Street and Garstang Road was known as Addison Road before being re-named Blackpool Road. It was the subject of a number of widening schemes, but in this view we see single lane traffic in each direction. It is believed the photo was taken from the upper storey of the Butchers' and Commercial Hotel that was located on the south east corner of Addison Road and Brook Street. Preston Motor Auctions are on the left of the image. The Auctions on the left is now Budget Exhausts & Tyres. The roads ahead to the left and to the right heading away from us are Norris Street and then Plungington Road.

© LEP

© LEP

Above A busy post-war traffic scene from Lancaster Road c1950. From the wall clock on the right, we can make out that it is early afternoon at 2.39pm. This was a pick-up and drop off point for many local bus routes and we can see five buses on the road in this picture. The shortage of buses in the immediate postwar period meant that many older vehicles were refurbished. These, however, appear to be from Leyland Motors, at the large factory within seven miles of Preston. Employing thousands of local people they were once the fifth largest producer of trucks and buses in the world.

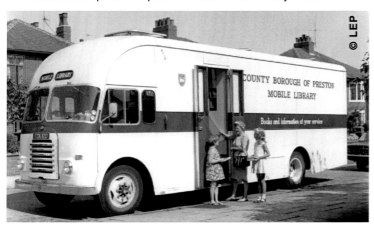

© LEP

Left: Mobile libraries are popular particularly with the elderly and infirm who are unable to get easily to their local branch for their renewal of books. The readers pictured here at the top of Winmarleigh Road, near Blackpool Road in Ashton, in 1969, are clearly of a younger age. At least the children in the picture enjoyed their diet of Enid Blyton's 'Famous Five' or such horsey tales as Mary O'Hara's 'My Friend. The Bedford SB vehicle, pictured, entered service in 1966. The mobile library service has been around longer than most people imagine. A 'perambulating' library in a horse drawn cart was established in Cumbria in 1857 with another founded in Warrington a year later.

WORK & INDUSTRY

Left and bottom left: Women far outnumber the men in this 1919 photograph of a group of cotton weavers at Centenary Mill in New Hall Lane, Preston. Centenary Mill was built by John Horrocks in the 1890s. Young people as young as twelve often went into the mills while still attending school part time. As they grew older they would work their way through a series of jobs within the mill, developing many skills in the textile industry and often staying in the same industry for the rest of their lives. Weavers learned to lip read when all the looms were running as the noise in the room was deafening and people found it impossible to hear each other speak. Centenary Mill was built on the site of New Preston Mill. It was finished in 1895 at a cost of £125,000. The property survives today in its new guise as an apartment complex.

Below: Everyone has heard of cotton spinning and wool fulling, but how many of us can say we also associate weaving with velvet? Yet, this was big business for J R and A Smith in 1922. The company employed a sizeable staff, as we see here. It had just received a massive boost to its efficiency by the installation of new engine power to its manufacturing process. The British Velvet and Plush Company, to give the firm its full name, operated from Manchester Mill, on Moseley Street, just off New Hall Lane. Whether crushed, hammered or embossed, velvet has been particularly important in upholstery and soft furnishing and is often associated with the nobility. King Richard II decreed in his will that his body should be clothed 'in velveto'.

Above: By the start of World War I, the textile industry in and around town was at its peak. It seemed that nearly every family had someone connected in some capacity with weaving or spinning. There were about 65 mills in operation and they provided the lifeblood of the local economy. The Tennyson Road Weaving Mill was just such a workplace. It is thought that this picture dates from 1902 and was possibly taken during the Preston Guild that was celebrated that year in its usual 20 year cycle. In the background, readers with good eyesight might be able to pick out the small American flag. Maybe this was a sort of 'thank you' message to the supplier of raw cotton to this mill.

exception, have hogged the front row. Even when women were fulfilling traditional male roles as the menfolk were serving in uniform overseas, most of those males left behind clung on to the top positions. The company was involved in textile engineering that included the manufacture of looms.

Right: In 1942, wartime slogans were everywhere. We were told 'to be like dad and keep mum' in order to maintain secrecy. Out on the land we were urged to 'dig for victory', with this lesser known maxim applying to industry, as seen displayed by the workforce at Gregson and Monk. Note how the men, with one token

R&E Bamford Limited
The Seeds of Enterprise

R&E Bamford Limited is a family run company now in its third generation. Manufacturers & Wholesalers to the pet trade, they offer an excellent range of pet products, specialising in quality racing pigeon, wild bird and cage and aviary foods.

The firm was founded in Bretherton in the 1920s by Robert Bamford. He had previously worked as a cotton weaver in Croston, where he met his wife to be, Mary Norris.

Robert opened premises in Marl Cop, as Corn Merchants, buying and selling grain, and milling. Marl House doubled as a bakery and grocery store staffed by Mary and her sister; it later incorporated the Post Office. Supplying poultry feed was the main activity, Robert later contracted threshing and baling jobs and provided labour for local farmers at harvest and hay time. Robert would travel to local farmers in his pony and trap collecting orders, and when delivering bags they often exceeded two hundredweight, almost six times heavier than today's standard size; little wonder that knee joint problems were common.

The business was staffed by Robert and his brother, until joined by his four sons, William, Harry, Ronald and Eric. William and Ronald were office-oriented, while their wives, Kitty and Bessie ran the grocery department. Harry (until he was killed in a motor bike accident) and Eric worked in the mill and on transport; Eric's wife Jean also worked in the grocery and bakery division.

By the 1950s staff numbers had built up to 20, but this number was reduced to six in the 1960s due to a national outbreak of fowl pest. During this time the family banded together to find new ways to keep the core business operating and emerged stronger for it.

The transition in trade and resulting expansion led the company to relocate in 1995 to a larger site at Globe Mill, Midge Hall, which was subsequently redeveloped into a bird food manufacturing plant.

Now under the guidance of the third generation of the founding family, Eric's sons, Alan and Philip manage the company, along with Company Secretary, Ronald's daughter, Joan. Bamfords acquired the Top Flight trade name and customer base from Spillers in 2000, establishing a national distribution network. The further acquisitions of the Quinastra label from Suffolk-based Muntons and pet wholesalers Nicholsons complemented the range.

Despite a serious fire in 2003, the company has continued to grow, with staff numbers now nearing 50. Most recently, the acquisition of on-line Wild Bird Food business, Soar Mill Seeds, has given the company an internet presence. The company now distributes nationally and has also stretched further afield to gain an international presence in Libya, Sweden and Kuwait.

Top left: *The old mill at Marl Cop in the 1930s.* **Left:** *Second generation of Bamford brothers – (left to right) Eric, Harry, William and Ronald, circa 1935.* **Centre:** *A receipt from 1940.* **Above:** *New Braby silos at Globe Mill, Midge Hall.*

E H Booth & Co. Ltd
A Shopping History

With its headquarters in Longridge Road, Ribbleton, the E H Booth grocery chain may not yet be the biggest name in the business, but the firm can certainly more than match its larger competitors when it comes to company history.

The firm of E H Booth & Co. Ltd was founded by Edwin Henry Booth, a man of outstanding character and exceptional ability. He was very proud of the business he had set up declaring that he sold the best goods he could buy, in shops staffed with first class assistants and that customers should not expect him to run after them.

When still a child Edwin's thrice-married mother and his step-father seem to have simply abandoned him in Bury.

In Edwin's own words his step-father was a "veritable monster whose sons followed his example and came to grief and premature death. In time the scoundrel became well known and had to leave the country, taking my poor mother with him. And I was left at about ten years of age to myself in this pitiless world."

Sheltered for a few months by an unsuccessful manufacturer in Bolton, Edwin eventually found a job as an errand boy for a tailor, earning three shillings (15p) a week. Three years later Edwin walked to Preston where he found a job working for a Mr Threlfall, a grocer based in Liverpool.

Acutely aware of his lack of education, and keen on self improvement, Edwin took to studying grammar and mathematics each evening, and each morning from 5am to 8am. And he also saved up.

Edwin Booth opened his first small shop, the China House, in Blackpool, in 1847.

The 'shop' was in fact an old barn. The owner of the barn, located in the main street, agreed to convert it into a shop at the cost of £20 in return for the promise of an annual rent of £15. A man was hired to fit up the shop, and yet another to decorate it. Mr Threfall, Edwin's previous employer, agreed to trust him with an advance of £80 worth of goods – a large sum at the time, equivalent to a workman's yearly income.

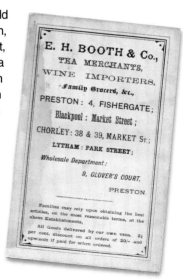

For the next three months Edwin worked flat out. With great joy he ended the period with a profit of £50! Edwin was just 19 years old, but he was on his way.

Edwin imported special French wines and brandies, and even chartered a ship to bring in a cargo of tea and other groceries for the opening of Preston Dock. When the first Electric Supply Company in Preston nearly failed he went to its rescue as he had faith in the future of electricity.

*Top: Edwin Henry Booth, the founder. **Left:** An early view of E H Booth & Co.'s Blackpool shop. **Above:** An early company brochure cover.*

By the time he died in 1899 Edwin Booth was one of the best-known men in the district around Preston. His early hardships had made him sympathetic to the poor and all in trouble. He had co-founded an orphanage, been treasurer for the Homes for the Blind and on the committee of the Royal Cross Trust for the deaf and dumb. While he lived, no good cause in Preston was left unanswered.

Edwin had put his four sons, each in turn, into the business, but Edwin junior left to take up the wholesale tea trade in London and Fred became a doctor, serving as Medical Officer of Health for St Anne's on Sea. The eldest, John, however, was of great help to him, becoming in 1881 a junior partner with his father and gradually taking over responsibility until, on the death of Edwin senior in 1899, he became chairman of the company.

The business had been made a private limited company three years before the founder's death. John Booth's co-directors were his youngest brother Tim and a faithful employee, William Tattersall.

In those early days sugar was bought in great casks and was generally dark in colour. Lump sugar came in tall white cones and there was a chopping machine for it, worked by a foot pedal. Soft soap came in kegs and a trick played on new boys was to tell them to put their fingers in and have a good taste!

Customers came in their carriages and the good housewife took a great interest in the quality and prices of goods. Long credit was taken, bills were often paid yearly or half yearly and it needed a stout-hearted grocer to stand out for his due.

'Mr John' the Chairman had been delicate as a boy, and in his youth was sent on a voyage to the Mediterranean. Visiting Greece and Turkey gave him a special interest in cargoes of currants and sultanas from ports he had visited.

On the occasion of his Golden Wedding all 349 members of staff wrote congratulations to John and his wife Ada. Their early married life had been spent at St Anne's but he had moved to Preston to be nearer his father. The couple lived at Barton Hall

where the staff were entertained on 'bonus day'. John Booth had begun a profit sharing scheme for the staff in 1909.

About 1900, a gown shop in Blackburn was bought and turned into another Booths store. It was decided to make the large upstairs rooms into the company's first cafe. People in those days did not have the cafe habit, but still the venture prospered. Later, property in Fishergate was bought, with further adjoining houses alongside gradually being added.

Top left: The magnificent Avenham Tower in Preston, home to Mr & Mrs Edwin Booth in their latter years. *Left:* Son of the founder, John Booth, and wife Ada with their children, Wyn and Connie in 1890. *Above:* Booths Blackburn store and café. *Below:* Booths shop and café, Fishergate, Preston, in the 1930s.

The 1960s would become a decade of ever-increasing success. All Booths' new business was in cash, so the firm moved to phase out the order trade by putting on a small delivery charge and then gradually increasing it. Delivery vans were gradually disposed of and credit eliminated. These new policies brought sales to £2 million by 1966.

Since existing resources were being used for conversion there were no new shops for a while. Ashton was unsuitable for conversion and was closed. To compensate a new store was opened in Woodplumpton Road.

Both 'Mr Wyn' and 'Mr Kenny', John Booth's sons, served in the armed forces during the First World War.

When the war was over Booths began acquiring local shops, the first two at Ashton and Leyland.

'Mr John' died in 1941, by which time his two elder sons, Mr Wyn and Mr Kenny, were well established in the business. They had been given responsibility from an early age and in due time became directors; meanwhile training up two of the fourth generation of Booths to join the family business had begun.

'Mr Kenny' died, aged 78, in July 1970. He had been with the company for 60 years. The new 'Mr John' succeeded as Chairman and work continued. Mr John had joined the company in 1946 and his brother, Michael, in 1947.

In 1971, the shop at Longton was rebuilt and extended.

In September 1973, Edwin J Booth joined the firm, representing the fifth generation of the Booth family.

Top left: Bonus Day gathering in the 1920s. Mr John pictured central and Mr Kenny and Mr Wyn are pictured at either end of the front row. Left: Mr Kenny Booth with his father John and sons Michael and John, 1920s. Centre: Booths Penwortham store in the 1930s. Below: Booths Fishergate store and café in the mid-1930s.

Following the company centenary in 1947 Booths continued to trade successfully in the traditional pattern. Mr Wyn died in 1951 and Mr Kenny succeeded him as Chairman. By the mid-Fifties sales had reached £1million, a notable figure for those days.

From the end of the Second World War until 1960, every year was a record year. Then came the challenge of the supermarket. Sales stopped increasing and since one third of business was on credit it was not possible to cut prices, though, of course, wages still had to rise. The year 1961 saw a 2% loss of trade. If Booths was to have a future it would have to be on a new basis.

Fulwood and Leyland were chosen as the company's first self-service stores. Customers told Mr Kenny, "You won't see me with a wire basket", and "You're making a dreadful mistake, Mr Booth", but in 1962 sales increases of 3% were announced with the two new self-service stores up by 20%. By 1963, Preston, the firm's most profitable store, had been successfully converted.

On the staff side, more attention was paid to the recruitment of well educated individuals under a trainer-manager scheme, so that the teams running the improved stores were second to none. Fresh meat became available in all stores, its ordering overseen by fresh meat controller Mr Smith who provided new skills to Booths' considerable previous experience.

The year 1975 saw the opening of the Garstang store. Later in that same year a very good acquisition was made. Looking for a replacement for the small though prosperous Fulwood store, Booths discovered that the asking price for the plot they wanted at Sharoe Green was £250,000. However, the vendor came under financial pressure and in 1974 agreed to accept just £42,000 provided the money was immediately available. It became the very first 'Booths' Shopping Centre' which set the style for future development. It opened in 1978.

Mr Simon Booth joined the firm in 1975, becoming a director in 1984. Already the Sharoe Green site had become too small for the very profitable trade there. The sales floor was enlarged and the fruit and vegetable area was much improved. Sharoe Green had become the leading store in both sales and profits. At this time it was decided to close the last of the Booths' cafes, that in Preston. With the decline in the popularity of 'afternoon' and 'high' tea, the cafe had simply become outdated.

In 1987, Mr Graham Booth joined the Board alongside his brother. The previous year was a record one with profits of £1,352,000. In 1988, however, the Preston store was closed. It had been losing business because of its lack of a car park. Waterstones, the booksellers, took over the shop but Booths' head office remained in Glover's Court.

Ten years later, in 1997, Booths built its first store in Yorkshire, at Ilkley. The company felt confident that it was able to please an increasing number of people who looked upon it as 'traditionally better'.

In June 2005, the company Chairman, the fifth generation of his family to lead the business, Edwin J Booth, was awarded the BITC (Business in the Community) Prince of Wales Ambassador Award for North West England. This is given to individuals whose leadership and commitment to responsible business practice and the actions they have taken personally have created a positive impact both inside their company and on the wider society.

Top left: Booths Lane Ends, Preston, store in 1963. **Centre and above:** *Vintage Booths delivery vans outside the company's Fishergate (left) and Ribbleton stores in the 1930s (left) and 1960s.* **Below:** *The changing face of E H Booth & Co., Longton. From l-r: 1927, 1963, 1982 and 2008.*

Remarkably, in the ten years between 1997 and 2007 the company had doubled in size. The number of employees had grown from 1,500 to almost 3,000, whilst sales had soared from £95 million in 1997 to £231 million in 2007.

Although the company has since closed its Leyland, Penwortham (Liverpool Road), South Shore, Lytham (Market Square) stores, and its oldest store in St. Annes, it continued to develop plans for new stores. These included two new Lancashire stores in Garstang and Hesketh Bank in 2007, and in January 2009, the Company announced it was to take a unit in the proposed redeveloped New Squares shopping centre in Hale Barns, Greater Manchester.

Booths achieved second place in the list of the World's Greatest Food Retailers in 2006. The panel of top designers, architects, analysts, journalists, suppliers and retailers was brought together by national trade publication, The Grocer, and asked to rank their favourite food retailers from anywhere in the world. They were impressed by the quality of the company's

In 2011, two new stores followed in MediaCity, Salford, and Penrith, Cumbria. More recently, Booths have also opened a new store in Milnthorpe in 2012 and Barrowford in 2014.

offer, its focus on local sourcing and head for innovation. Simon Bell, retail director of foodservice firm Leathams, voted Booths' Chorley store first above Selfridges in London. He applauded its excellent customer service, knowledge of products and friendly staff.

That same year a new head office was opened in Ribbleton, Preston, and includes environmentally friendly features, such as using rainwater to flush the toilets.

Top left: The Operating Board, 2008. From left to right: Diane Pickup, Graham Booth, David Benson, Edwin Booth, Simon Booth, John Vandermeer, Andrew Rafferty and Chris Dee. Bottom left: Michael Booth welcomes HRH Prince Charles to Booths' Kendal premises in March 2008. Left and below: The old and the modern, Booths Chorley in the 1930s and 2008.

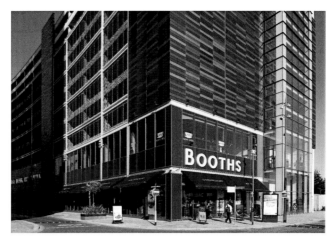

The company's latest development is for a new 35,000 sq ft supermarket at The Teanlowe Centre, in Poulton-le-Fylde, due to open in 2015.

Meanwhile, committed to supporting small-scale suppliers, Booths launched their New Supply Website in 2012. This is a dedicated website for prospective suppliers to apply to be a supplier of Booths supermarkets. It was followed by their first 'Meet The Buyer Day', in August 2012, with those suppliers who had applied online given the opportunity to pitch their products to Booths buyers. The events proved very successful and have become a firm fixture in the Booths calendar. Since its launch over 40 new suppliers have being listed.

2012 also saw a 6th generation of the family, Henry Booth, son of Graham Booth, join the business as Graduate Trainee. Henry will spend his first two years training to be a Buyer. "It's a great pleasure to be able to welcome a member of the 6th generation into the business. Henry will learn the skills of retailing from the bottom up interacting with people at all levels of the business" said Chairman Edwin J Booth.

The Company continues to be controlled by the Booth family although shares are also held by employees under a scheme that was started by John Booth in 1920.

By any measure Booths is an extraordinary undertaking with an extraordinary history. It is wholly unusual for a family firm to thrive over such a long period in what is notoriously one of the most competitive business sectors – the retail grocery trade. 'Clogs to clogs in three generations' is the usual fate of family businesses created by one inspired but impoverished founder. E H Booth & Co. Ltd, however, is the exception which proves the rule.

Today, nearly 170 years since its founding, the firm is looking forward to the future with confidence, a confidence built on the firm foundations laid down by Edwin Henry Booth so very long ago.

Top left, both pictures: *Booths Garstang (top) and Penrith stores.* ***Centre and top right:*** *Interior and exterior views of Booths new MediaCity, Salford, store.* ***Below:*** *Booths headquarters in Longridge Road, Ribbleton. Photographs © David Millington Photography Ltd*

J. Wareing & Son (Wrea Green) Ltd
A Century of Progress

Fylde Scout heaquarters in St. Annes, a new showroom and workshop for Chapelhouse Motors in Southport, a 626 ton steelwork structure for Lytham Quays luxury apartments development and 200 tons of steelwork fabricated to build the new mosque and cultural centre at Wimberley Street in Blackburn, a building constructed in two phases spread over three years.

Whether it is sports halls or potato stores which are asked for, Wareings has built them all and it has been doing so for a very long time indeed.

The business was founded in 1909 by two brothers, wheelwrights and joiners George and James Wareing. The Wareings provided a huge range of services to farmers in and around Wrea Green, not just cart wheels for the horse-drawn vehicles then still used in their thousands but the hundreds of different items which were still within living memory and normally crafted from wood. These included feeding troughs, barn doors, feed barriers, fences and hen huts.

Prefabricated steel-clad buildings almost define the closing decades of the 20th century. When did the first one appear? Who can say, but such buildings have slowly and inexorably changed the urban landscape in the way that Accrington brick did in the 19th century. No matter where you go in Britain, you are seldom out of sight of at least one of these buildings which astonishingly seem to be able to spring up in days. Preston's J. Wareing & Son (Wrea Green) Ltd, now based Whinbrick Works, Blackpool Road, Kirkham, is today well known all over Lancashire and far beyond, as a firm specialising in the erection of steel framed buildings. In fact, the firm's reputation extends much further than the north-west and the company has supplied buildings to places as far afield as the Falkland Islands and the Sudan as well as the many islands off mainland Britain.

Top left: The only photograph that exists of co-founder George Wareing, extreme right, behind the lady in the black. Left: James Wareing, circa 1910. Bottom left: An early picture taken at Smithy Fold showing horse-drawn vehicles with shafts and newer rubber wheeled carts. Below: James Wareing (with his back to the camera) and Jack Marshall in the workshop.

Nor has the firm restricted itself to supplying simple corrugated metal sheds and warehouses: at Wareings the firm's main asset is its adaptability, being able to produce whatever the customer needs as economically as possible. Such flexibility has resulted in the firm obtaining contracts for buildings ranging from the

But as farming methods changed over the years so did the firm's products, not least with an increasing concentration on prefabricated farm buildings. Of course, the material of choice was still wood and Wareings' timber cow kennels, for example, would become a familiar sight on farms up to a hundred miles from Preston.

Eldest brother, George, was highly religious, a devoted worshipper at Wrea Green Church and was never known to swear. James by contrast was later described as 'something of a character'. He was never afraid to speak his mind – not least when involved in a dispute over payment for the timber for the new memorial lych-gate at St Nicholas' Church, built to honour the dead in the First World War. In the end the timber was funded by the Wareings themselves.

In 1930, James' son Harry Matthew joined the business to work alongside his father and uncle. Like them Harry served his time as an apprentice joiner, whilst also assisting with the accounting.

Every Saturday morning young Harry would help his Uncle George with the book keeping. This ritual would take place at George's house with a break at mid-morning to listen to the short church service on the wireless. The service was always welcomed by Harry as it signalled a much deserved tea break and a short reprieve from the figures.

Following an accident in 1936 George decided to retire from the business, though he would live on until his death in 1962.

Harry now took over the administration of the firm, and the name of the company changed to J Wareing & Son. The business, however, continued to function in much the same way as it had since it was founded in 1909 with woodwork remaining the primary focus of activity.

After the end of the Second World War in 1945, in order to encourage farmers to produce more food the Government provided grants to help fund modern buildings. This marked the beginnings of Wareing steel-framed construction. In Glasgow a company had begun to manufacture angle iron roof trusses. Wareings decided to use these on three buildings, two of which

are still in use today. On seeing how easy and simple the process was the company decided to make their own.

Until the early 1960s, Wareings had three teams of men erecting buildings within Lancashire. Major estates such as the Duchy of Lancaster, the Church Commission of England and the Holker Estates, along with local Water Authorities, became important customers, as well as many individual farmers.

Top left: A post-war Wareing's Morris commercial wagon fully loaded with two 40' x 18' poultry cabins. *Top right:* An early example of Wareing construction of a clear span portal roof frame type building. *Left:* Harry and Phyllis Wareing in 1971 when Harry was Chairman of the then Fylde Rural & District Council. *Below:* One of Wareing's erecting teams of the 1960s.

The demand for buildings began to outstrip Wareings' production capacity and a decision was made to expand the business. By the 1970s, the workforce had grown to over 60 with some six erection gangs.

Harry's sons Peter and Andrew had now joined the family firm. Andrew Wareing, together with Oliver Gillett and John Alston, looked after the manufacture, transportation and erection of buildings. Peter Wareing, together with Peter Bunce and Geoff Wilby, looked after the sales side of the business.

Meanwhile, following the loss of his wife Elizabeth in 1954, James had continued to work part time. In the late 1960s, however, he decided to hang up his tools and retire for good. After a long and restful retirement he passed away in 1975 at the grand age of 89.

A big selling point of the Wareings' buildings was that they could be made and delivered in kit form for erection on site. That experience would pay major dividends for the business in the long run. By the early 1970s, it was evident that a sea change was in progress. The firm's catalogue still featured wooden cow kennels but new materials, corrugated roofing, steel pillars and asbestos sheeting were clearly pushing the older material out.

By the 1980s, warehouses and industrial units on industrial estates were often being described as 'barn like'. It was an accurate reflection of their origins. Building prefabricated dairy units, storage buildings and cow kennels for agricultural clients provided the skills and expertise for Wareings to begin to offer its services to the industrial sector. As pioneers of 'kit' building the firm was now able to offer new customers a specialised service. Fabricated to individual requirements with a choice of many types of cladding, kits could be provided complete with instructions enabling customers to erect their own buildings using their own or local labour.

The company would soon be producing up to fifteen prefabricated buildings each week, two thirds of which would be provided in kit form. Sadly, Harry Wareing passed away in 2000 at the age of 84. Today, the firm is run by his two sons Peter and Andrew, helped by a staff of over 70 including five of Harry's grandchildren.

Top: A Wareing 45' x 30' kit building exhibited at the Great Yorkshire Show where the company have had a stand since the 1960s. Centre: Structural steel work totalling 626 tons forming the frame for a block of luxury apartments at Lytham Quays. Included in the project was the design of steel work and assistance with the design of the foundations. Left: A Wareing family photograph, 2009.

The new 10-acre site houses the most modern machinery and technology. The joiners' shop is pristine with not a speck of sawdust in sight. Steel framed buildings are manufactured using the latest computerised cutting and drilling machinery. Company founders George and James Wareing would be amazed.

Today, the company's bespoke structures are used in many different applications from livestock buildings and stables to retail units and industrial premises.

Robin Wareing began working for the firm in 1983, and in 1987 his sister Sally joined too. Peter's youngest son Neil soon joined his brother and sister in the business. Andrew's sons Christopher and Richard soon followed suit.

The large staff of fully-trained people enables the company to fabricate steelwork to produce a variety of building types whilst an in-house joinery department, an echo of the firm's early origins, still manufactures many products from wood including doors and window frames.

In 2007, J Wareing & Son (Wrea Green) Ltd moved less than a mile away from its original base in Wrea Green to its present location at Whinbrick Works where a modern, practical and efficient working environment was created. Phase 2 of the project was completed in 2008.

The firm offers clients, both in the UK and internationally, tailor made solutions to meet their specific requirements – whether it be basic steel-frame and cladding, steel structures in kit format or complete design and build packages as well as re-cladding and over-cladding of existing buildings. With more than a century behind it the company is now looking forward to another century ahead of it.

Top: J. Wareing & Son (Wrea Green) Ltd's new spacious modern site. *Left:* Recent projects: a Giraffe House at Blackpool Zoo and Blackburn Mosque. *Below:* The entire Wareing staff pictured in 2009, the company's centenary year.

BAKO NW - The Key Ingredient to the Food Industry

BAKO North Western, based on Roman Way Industrial Estate, Longridge Road, is one of Preston's most important businesses and in 2014 will reach its 50th year of trading.

The company has grown remarkably since the early Sixties when several independent craftsmen bakers decided to form a buying co-operative called North Western Bakers. Its aim would be to provide all bakers in the area with high quality ingredients, more competitively priced through buying in bulk and splitting pallets into smaller quantities, more suited to the needs of a baker.

The co-operative began life in a small office in Warrington, registered on the 28 December, 1964. The first storage facility was a tiny warehouse in New Hall Lane, Preston. A move came just two years later, to a converted mill in Ribbleton Lane, Preston. However, the building's age and condition meant

Craftsman bakers buying together, growing together.

that the company spent a lot of time and money on maintenance. With such high overheads, it seemed prudent to consider a further move to purpose-built premises.

On the advice of the Central Lancashire Development Corporation, the company looked at Roman Way Industrial Estate and subsequently built 20,000 sq ft of warehousing, loading bays and offices. Following the move to Roman Way, the Directors of the business (all practising craftsmen bakers) decided a name change was in order, and so BAKO North Western was born.

Within five years, the company had added a further 10,000 square feet of warehousing and continued to grow by adding additional office accommodation, together with a six-hundred pallet chilled and frozen storage facility.

Today, the company remains true to its origins, still operating for and on behalf of its traditional customer base of Craftsman Bakers and Confectioners, while having also expanded into the foodservice industry, having been successful in winning a number of local authority tenders.

BAKO North Western's customers are supplied with a wide choice of over 2,000 products. These range from traditional staple goods such as fats, sugar and chocolate, to high quality finished goods such as sausage rolls and doughnuts.

Left: A North Western Bakers Ltd brochure from the 1970s.
Above: A company exhibition in the early 1970s.

The development of its range of own label products has been a major focus in recent years developing from simple commodity items, with the first being lard 25 years ago, to more complicated products such as cake mixes and muffins. This reflects both the expansion of its customer base and also the change in the baking industry, which require both time saving and continually consistent products.

Its next challenge, having reached the milestone of 50 years, is the execution of its ambitious plans to celebrate the year with a number of competitions and events, to reward staff and customers alike for their support.

Service is of huge importance and so handling and delivery of goods is both efficient and prompt, managed using BAKO's computerised warehouse management system. Appropriate, multi-temperature wagons transport goods to customers in prime condition.

The company's commitment to quality and high service levels is reflected by its association with the Institute of Customer Services which has led to the recent employment of a full time Customer Care Executive who is on hand to handle any enquiry. The company's Quality systems ensure that continual improvement is maintained. The company is accredited to several Quality Standards, including ISO9001:2008 used as a management tool and B.R.C. Storage & Distribution. More recently, the company has also gained the environmental accreditation ISO14001:2004, committing itself to viewing its presence in the community in a sustainable and socially responsible way. The business has already exceeded its target to reduce its energy and paper consumption but will continue to pursue improvements for the next five years.

BAKO North Western now boasts a workforce of 150, including buyers and marketers, who continue to innovate and push the company forward. Plans are currently in place to expand into the adjacent land at Roman Way, to extend the yard facilities and increase freezer capacity.

Top left: Making deliveries in the late 1980s. **Above:** The current warehouse facility at Roman Way. **Below:** BAKO's 50 years in the industry anniversary banner.

CELEBRATING 50 YEARS IN THE INDUSTRY

Huntapac
Deep Roots

Huntapac Produce Ltd, based in the village of Tarleton, in Lancashire, laid down its roots during wartime Britain of 1942. Since then the business has become one of the UK's leading growers of carrots and parsnips, supplying retailers and markets across the UK. From a modest start, over 70 years ago, the company now employs some 500 staff.

Huntapac Produce Ltd was founded by William Hunter Snr who set out with the ambition to supply Lancashire markets with home-grown, nutritious root vegetables, a vital part of the staple - and healthy - diet for people during the war period when food production and distribution was a key component of the nation's war effort on the home front.

The business has always been on the same site, Blackgate Lane, in Tarleton. Since its founding, expansion and redevelopment of the original site has taken place a number of

times. At present, even more work is in progress to increase its cold storage facility by 100%. This development is expected to be completed in 2014.

The firm's main customers are UK based. Leading supermarket chains, convenience retail chains, food service companies and markets across the UK are supplied by Huntapac with local Preston based companies, such as Booths and James Hall & Co. Ltd, being customers for many years.

Today, the company supplies a wide range of root vegetables, salads and brassicas. Deliveries are made 24 hours a day, seven days a week all across the UK in one of 57 Huntapac articulated vehicles.

Above: A young Bill Hunter, today's Chairman, on one of the company tractors in 1955, aged 14. Below left: William Hunter's 1950s Seddon. Below: Staff take a break from harvesting to pose for the camera, 1962.

Huntapac Produce Ltd is unique as it grows carrots the length and breadth of the UK with new season carrots being grown on land in Suffolk and throughout the year working up the country through Shropshire, Yorkshire, Lancashire and then finishing off the season in Inverness, Scotland.

Throughout the UK season Huntapac also grows its own brassicas such as cabbage, cauliflower and broccoli, salads such as iceberg, little gem and romaine, and then in a very tiny window of opportunity lasting just six weeks asparagus is also grown in Hightown near Formby.

As technology has significantly changed over the years, Huntapac has also moved with the times which has increased the efficiency and output of the business. Machinery such as 'carrot polishers' and 'parsnip trimmers' have improved overall efficiency and camera graders, which automatically grade carrots, removing any imperfect ones from the those being packed. Yet some things never change; no technology can fully replace the human eye and staff are still employed to oversee the final product.

Most recently, Huntapac Produce has entered the snacking market for the first time with the launch of its own brand of crisps. 'Roots' Vegetable Crisps are made from Huntapac's carrots,

parsnips and beetroot and are an extension of the producer's Roots-branded salad and vegetable bags.

The company is also heavily involved with the local community, not only as a major employer but also in its promotional work with local schools, raising awareness of the younger generation to the benefits of healthy eating and the important place of vegetables in their diets. 'Colin the Carrot' usually makes an appearance making the visit informative and fun.

Today, the business is in the hands of Chairman Bill Hunter and William Hunter's grandsons, Warren and Jason Hunter, as well as a fourth generation - Warren's two sons who have recently joined the business.

In 1942, when the nation was in danger of being slowly starved to death by the action of German U-boats, home-grown food helped Britain win the war. Seven decades on, Huntapac is now helping Britain win the campaign for healthy eating.

Top: No more aching backs for the staff as William Hunter rolls out his new invention, a cauliflower harvesting machine, 1966. *Centre:* Chairman, Bill Hunter and sons Jason, Director (left), and Warren, Managing Director (right). **Left and above:** The old and the new - a vintage Hunter delivery truck (left) and one of Huntapac's modern articulated vehicles.

Kirkham Grammar School

The educational world seems to change every day as new initiatives are introduced, yet a good education is an enduring benefit. Some of our best educational establishments have survived the turmoil of changes in current trends whether it be Academies or free schools. Kirkham Grammar School is such an institution, enjoying a history and tradition that dates back to the 16th century or even beyond.

Centuries of Christian tradition underpin the education provided by Kirkham Grammar School, which was founded as a charity school in 1549 and consequently celebrated its 450th anniversary in 1999.

Indeed, the school's roots can be traced back even further than the reign of Henry VIII's short-lived son Edward VI, to the chantry school attached to St Michael's Church, Kirkham, as long ago as the 13th century. It was there in the church grounds that the school remained until it moved to occupy its present site on Ribby Road in 1911.

Back in 1585, however, during the reign of Queen Elizabeth the First, the Thirty Men of Kirkham, a group which administered parish business, took over responsibility for the school. It appears they did not always perform their duties particularly well for by the early part of the 17th century the school had fallen into disrepair and had been without a master for seven years.

Remarkably, Isabell Birly, a humble alehouse keeper, came to the rescue in 1621 when she presented the Thirty Men of Kirkham with £30 in her apron for the school's restoration.

Although £30 was a substantial amount of money in the 17th century, it was not enough to keep a school running. In 1655, however, Henry Colburn, an old boy of the school, left land and a large sum of money to the school in his will, putting it in the trust of the Company of Drapers in London. Then began a long and cherished partnership between the company and the school which has continued to the present day, though the Drapers surrendered control of the school in 1944 after having endowed it with large and impressive extensions in 1938. The connection with the Drapers is recalled in the school crest; on the shield are the doves of Kirkham township together with the triple coronets of the Drapers' Company.

Top left: *The school crest and its motto, 'Ingredere Ut Proficias' – 'Enter in order to profit'.* **Above:** *The school tapestry showing Isabell Birly in her apron and presenting the Thirty Men of Kirkham with £30 for the restoration of the school.* **Below:** *The school in 2014.*

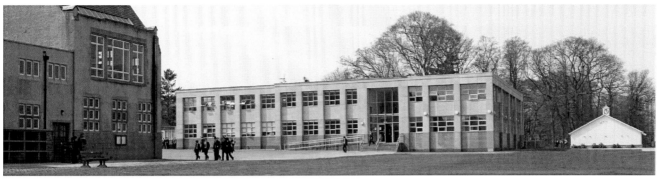

Independent status ceased temporarily in 1944 when the school became a voluntary aided boys' grammar school. A further major building extension, the Norwood Science Building, was opened in 1965, and itself subsequently extended later. In 1979, the Board of Governors took the bold decision to revert to independent status and Kirkham Grammar School admitted girls to become a co-educational school for the first time in its history.

During the last twenty five years the school has had a remarkable period of development. Rapid growth in pupil numbers has seen the school grow from a predominately boys' school of just over 300 to a fully co-educational school of nearly 950 pupils, becoming the largest independent school on the Fylde. This development has seen the school develop its own Junior School on a modern purpose-built site adjacent to the Senior School. Pupils are now admitted from the age of three and most continue their education at school until 18. One of the key features in this period of growth was a partnership with BAE Systems, which helped the school design and build its modern Technology Centre, since designated as an International School of Excellence.

The traditional listed buildings remain intact with a beautiful façade to the school which provides a strong focus for visitors and pupils alike. The older buildings have retained their impact with a small boarding house still intact with nearly 70 boarders. The Old Hall provides the school with a traditional heart; a setting that is utilised well but which is beautifully set amidst oak panelling and longstanding honours boards. Around this traditional heart, however, has developed a thoroughly modern school with newly developed science facilities, a dedicated drama studio, floodlit all weather surface and recently opened new teaching rooms and offices along with day room space for the pupils. Such modern developments provide the school with outstanding facilities and its pupils with opportunities that are wide and varied.

Kirkham Grammar School's new Headmaster, Mr Richard Laithwaite, is a member of the Headmaster and Headmistresses' Conference which represents the 253 leading independent schools in the UK.

Today, Kirkham Grammar School is one of the leading schools in the North West with an enviable reputation for academic excellence combined with a national reputation for its sport. Drama and music have benefited recently from new building projects and the school has ambitious plans for the future.

*Top: The school's new Science Centre, Waite Building and Drama Studio. **Above left and below:** Pupils show off their prowess at music and sport.*

Lunar Caravans
Four Decades Down the Road

Lunar Caravans Ltd, based in Sherdley Road, Lostock Hall, Preston, is a firm whose name has become synonymous with the joy of the open road.

The Lunar story reflects more than forty years of passion and pride for building caravans that are undoubtedly the best in lightweight luxury touring. From humble beginnings, co-founders Brian Talbot and Ken Wilcock named their caravan manufacturing business Lunar following inspiration from the 1969 mission to land on the moon. They knew their caravans were exceptional but couldn't have imagined the size that Lunar has become today.

A two-berth caravan named the 'Saturn' was the firm's very first offering. Priced at £398 it made its appearance in July 1969.

From the flagship 'Clubman' to the legendary little 'Ariva', through the years the Lunar ethos has remained constant: build lightweight, high quality caravans with luxurious interiors. Protecting the firm's heritage and future has always been paramount.

The company was sold to a European manufacturer in the 1990s. There was, however, to be an even more important milestone in the company's history when a management buyout, led by Chairman and CEO, Brian Mellor, was finalised in 2007. At the end of 2007 the holding company The Tirus Group went into liquidation with fears that the successful Lunar brand might come to an end.

However, the buyout headed by Brian Mellor put the Preston based company firmly back into UK hands.

The economic downturn at the end of 2008 was a major challenge for the new management, a challenge met with models such as the 'Quasar 546' providing a family of six a fixed bunk bed single-axled layout at less than 1500 kgs loaded. Lunar also added more luxury to its top selling ranges 'Clubman' and the twin-axled 'Delta' ranges. Combined with lightweight and luxury fittings these proved top sellers for the company, bucking the economic trend and increasing Lunar's sales.

Lunar also produced its first time buyers 'Zenith' range, another lightweight value for money package, bringing Lunar Quality to this market sector. Most recently, 'Zeniths' have been replaced by the next generation entry level lightweight 'Venus' range.

Listening to customers and welcoming feedback, Lunar has developed its latest ranges with distinctive aerodynamic profiles, presenting some of the best looking tourers in Europe today. With new production processes, including the new CORE development process, and the introduction of its first motorhome since 2007, the Mercedes Sprinter based Landstar, Lunar's strategy is firmly in place. Providing value, quality and lightweight touring caravans from its Preston base for 45 years, Lunar Caravans continues to go from strength to strength.

Top: Lunar's first caravan, the two berth Saturn. Centre left: The 1979 Lunar Clubman which came with hot water, shower, oven, heater, fridge and double glazed plastic windows. Left: The luxurious and spacious interior of a 2014 Lunar Clubman SE. Above: The Lunar Quasar 564, which won first place in the Best Lightweight Caravan category at the 2014 Caravan Awards.

Pakawaste Ltd
Never Wasting an Opportunity

Pakawaste Ltd, based in Rough Hey Road, Preston, is the market leader in waste handling equipment. It was formed in 1976 by John Hunt.

In the intervening years waste and waste handling have become important public issues. Gone are the days when unwanted materials, whether domestic or industrial, was simply, and cheaply, carted off to a landfill site – and once out of sight was out of mind. Today, waste disposal and recycling have become a normal part of life – and the specialist equipment to deal with waste has become essential.

Pakawaste offers the largest range of waste handling equipment in the UK. Products range from static to portable compactors, vertical balers, horizontal balers, transfer stations, office shredders, bins and bin equipment and a variety of other specialist waste handling systems at its purpose-built factory in Preston. In addition to comprehensive range of standard waste handling products, Pakawaste's expert technical team can engineer bespoke and turnkey solutions to any waste problems which clients may be facing.

Pakawaste employs a team of service engineers who are based at strategic locations throughout the UK, ensuring unrivalled after sales service.

The company supplies a wide range of market sectors, including food processors and manufacturers, hotels and restaurants, supermarkets, shopping centres, hospitals, the pharmaceutical industry, logistics companies, manufacturing industries, educational establishments, waste contractors and recycling companies.

Pakawaste also has three other divisions: System Rental, which offers Pakawaste's premier waste handling equipment for hire or short/long term lease, Municipal Hire, which offers interim to long term hire of its range of municipal self-drive vehicles, and Engineering Services, which provides unrivalled levels of after sales service, preventative maintenance and response support service. Pakawaste has also been instrumental in several major individual projects including a development in Hong Kong.

In total Pakawaste has supplied over 7,000 waste handling systems throughout the UK and worldwide. The company has a turnover of £6.5m and employs 55 staff.

In July 2013, John Hunt, the Chairman of the Pakawaste Group, retired. The company was subsequently acquired by Group Managing Director, David Hamer, along with American investors. The investors have a wealth of experience within the waste management sector and already have a market leading rental business which has been established in the UK for many years.

Top left and below: *Pakawaste Ltd's Rough Hey Road premises.* *Left:* *A Pakawaste Extractpack, the first baler of its kind to combine baling and draining out-of-date beverage containers in one step.* *Above:* *A Pakawaste Portakrush 1000, one of the most popular portable compactors in the Portakrush range.*

Sika Limited
Global Technology Meets Local Expertise

Sika began in 1910 when the Gotthard rail tunnel running through the Swiss Alps required a secure waterproof system. It was Kaspar Winkler who developed and provided a completely new solution for chemically waterproofing cement mortars and concretes. Since then the company has gone from strength to strength and today Sika is the global technology and market leader in specialty chemicals for construction and industry. Sika has local businesses on all continents around the world and is well established in more than 76 countries.

Sika Limited, the UK subsidiary of the worldwide Sika Group, was established in 1927 to produce and market a wide range of technologically advanced systems. This activity is underpinned by unrivalled innovation in product development, the highest standards of manufacturing and renowned technical advice and in-situ guidance. Pioneers of a fully integrated service, the company is renowned for providing for end users or their specifiers, be they clients, designers, engineers, producers, distributors, merchants or contractors.

Sika Limited, based at Sika House, Miller Street, Preston, is an innovative manufacturer of products and solutions for the construction industry. Its Preston facility produces cold-applied coatings and membranes for roofs, walls and hygiene control.

Originally established in 1963 as Liquid Plastics, 50 years on the company continues to provide systems that are at the leading edge in their field, and are also durable, cost-effective and require minimal maintenance.

The company's extensive product range has been used in projects from the Arctic Circle to the heat of the Persian Gulf, and is regularly relied upon by many major organisations including British Airways, Marks & Spencer, Debenhams and the National Exhibition Centre (NEC) in Birmingham.

The reputation Sika has for quality and reliability is virtually unmatched, illustrated through a comprehensive portfolio of problem solving products that have been employed for many years in wide diversity of applications.

Sika is a pioneer in technological innovations designed to meet global challenges, and their Research & Development departments operate on a global scale with regional facilities located around the world.

Top left: Sika's Preston based offices. *Left:* The new Research & Development Centre under construction. *Above:* Working hard in the research laboratory.

Chris Miller
All Roads Lead to the Sea

A Gentleman's motor cruiser ready for a road trip, outside the Dock Offices on Watery Lane.

Chris Miller's crane lifts Donald Campbell's 'Bluebird' at Coniston.

Chris Miller's vehicles have been serving local industry for over 175 years. As a regular haulier for the Port of Preston it's perhaps not surprising that they were asked to carry the odd boat, but the company's founders could not have imagined how boat transport would shape the future of the family firm.

In the 1970s as the Port of Preston wound down, the fifth Chris Miller at the wheel of the family haulage business saw an opportunity to develop a new leisure facility for the town, and in 1983 co-organised the 'Aquaganza', a three-day event on the derelict dock which was designed to show the recreational benefits of the site.

The 'Manxman' comes to Preston and the dock basin changes from a port to a leisure destination.

Freighters gave way to leisure boats and the Port of Preston became Preston Marina, created and managed by Preston Marine Services Ltd, a new enterprise and sister company in which the awkward load handling and transport skills of Chris Miller Preston Ltd. continue to play a major role.

Below: Chris Miller's Guild 2012 float showing lifting technology across the firms' long history.

ACKNOWLEDGMENTS

The publishers would like to sincerely thank the following individuals and organisations for their help and contribution to this publication.

Lancashire Evening Post - www.lep.co.uk

With particular thanks to Mike Hill, Associate Editor

Mirrorpix - www.mirrorpix.com

Lancashire County Library and Information Services, Preston.

Lancashire Lantern Image Archive - www.lantern.lancashire.gov.uk

Steve Halliwell - Pubs in Preston - http://pubsinpreston.blogspot.co.uk

The Preston Digital Archive Team - www.flickr.com/photos/22711538@N07/

dusashenka's photostream - www.flickr.com/photos/oldcinemaphotos/

Blackburn with Darwen Library and Information Service

A.E. Shaw Preston Collection

www.blackburn.gov.uk/libraries